AMERICA'S FIRST FEMALE PRESIDENT...
2016?

AMERICA'S FIRST FEMALE PRESIDENT... 2016?

MOMS TAKE CHARGE

DR. THOMAS E. DAVIS,
COLONEL, USA (RET)

DEDICATION

This small token of my appreciation is dedicated to all the fantastic women who have so enriched my life, all the while preparing me to become a champion of sorts for them. For so many years, I have been witness to that misogynistic behavior by the almighty male of the species. I have been witness to multiple instances of very capable women being passed over "because they can't handle this kind of responsibility."

Conversely, I was also witness to so many instances where the females excelled when given the chance. I was never witness to abject failure among any of the women with whom I had the distinct pleasure of serving, either in the military or in the areas of medical and dental education. One lady in particular was the victim of that most insidious of all biases: gender bias.

Dr. Christine Haycock was one of those talented people who would not take no for an answer. Christine graduated from nursing school, later attended medical school, became a first-rate surgeon and teacher. Christine was a superb athlete as well as physician and educator and a military commander who was passed over for a slot that would have led to her becoming a general officer. Christine passed away in 2010. I will always miss her and her sage advice. She is a lady worth emulating. The reader can find more on Dr. Christine Haycock at the Library of the University of Medicine /Dentistry of NJ.

I further dedicate this work to all those ladies who aspire to be something more. especially to young ones like the little lady appearing on an episode of *Jeopardy!* who, when asked by Alex Trebek, "And what do you want to be when you grow up?" Her immediate and unhesitating response was, "I am going to be the President of the United States of America." So, to all you young and not-so-young ladies, go for it; take it if you must. You have been too long denied.

ACKNOWLEDGMENT

No individual can claim sole credit for a book. I engaged Tate Publishing of Mustang, Oklahoma, to guide me through the process. Their success in the past gives me hope that my small effort will meet some success, not necessarily in terms of revenue, but in terms of changing some attitudes, some practices with regard to our view of women.

It is with utmost gratitude that I wish to thank the following people.

1. Congresswoman Michele Bachmann of Minnesota, simply by thanking me for my support of women—particularly in the political arena—and giving me the final impetus to push this project to a productive conclusion.

2. Alice Paul, a Quaker maiden small in stature but huge in fortitude. She was my guiding spirit throughout this effort and continues to be an inspiration. Alice was nearly singularly responsible for the passage of the Nineteenth Amendment, and a most valiant effort to bring about passage of the Equal Rights Amendment.

3. Vida Ann Kerr Davis, my paternal grandmother, teacher, pioneer into the Indian territories of Oklahoma and learned to speak the Indian languages of each of the five civilized tribes—Cherokee, Choctaw, Chickasaw, Creek, and Seminole—and then founded a school to teach

Indian boys English, reading, writing, ciphering, and civics.

4. Inez Ethel Hupp Davis, my mother, for all the obvious reasons. She graduated in 1918 at the top of her high school class, followed two yeas later, graduating from Colorado Northern State Normal School with a teaching certificate. She was also one of the first women to be appointed postmistress. She is truly a role model extraordinaire.

5. Pearl Etha Williams Hupp, my aunt, teacher, and the first Town Marshal of Jackson Hole, Wyoming.
http://www.jacksonholehistory.org/history/characters/

6. Lou Fisher, instructor, novelist of the Long Ridge Writers Group, for his expertise, encouragement, and downright honesty. Sorry, Lou, I will never write that best-selling novel.

7. Carmela Catherine "Connie" Vaticano Davis, my wife of sixty-six plus years, for nourishing my body and soul. Daughter Patricia Ann was and is a generous bonus.

8. And most especially, the United States Army for giving me the opportunity to serve my beloved country for so many great years (1943–1985).

CONTENTS

PURPOSE OF THE BOOK

This old man is appalled to near consternation by the lack of a thorough education in civics received by my one daughter and by my three granddaughters in the public school system. I have decided, in some fashion, to attempt to rectify the situation. I will not bore you with the details that brought me to the realization that my kids and your kids were being literally defrauded by the public school system.

The system is fraught with misinformation about many things, mainly about our true beginnings as a nation. There is a plethora of misinformation being foisted off into the receptive minds of our youngest children by poorly trained educators. They are being forced to teach some unethical ideas fostered out by our ideological enemies. In very plain English, teachers' unions with pressure from the United States Department of Education have taken God out of the classrooms, have denigrated the deeds of our forefathers, and have or are attempting to introduce un-Christian behavioral ideals into malleable minds.

The very fact that Christmas must now be referred to as just a holiday rather than the celebration of the birth of Jesus Christ is abominable. The falsehoods being bandied about the United States not being founded as a Christian nation and that George Washington was not a Christian should have every American up in arms. Though George Washington is not known to have partaken in Holy Communion, he attended Presbyterian, Quaker, and Catholic services.

It is my intention to share the truth with all Americans. If the truth is unpalatable to anyone, let them leave on the first covered wagon. Political correctness is wrong, destructive, and far past any foreseeable usefulness. The term *political correctness* conjures up very bad feelings. The first word, *political*, is today a true pejorative that is ameliorated depending upon the noun it modifies. Should an individual be described as a political animal, it connotes an individual whose every act depends on the political considerations involved and the accompanying deviousness. It follows then that political correctness has a devious component.

The educator who falls into the trap of political correctness (rather than being a little more expansive by taking the time to give a more thorough explanation) is doing a great disservice to the student. Let me give an example or two.

Let's take the aforementioned case of George Washington. The lazy teacher will state, "George Washington was not a Christian because he claimed to follow no one particular religion." The statement is true, but the connotation is erroneous. General Washington, as has been documented, prayed often and fervently for guidance and providence from Almighty God. He was classified by many who knew him as a deist. He believed in God, but not necessarily in the same fashion as did Martin Luther or the Puritans. By every measure, George Washington was a devout Christian. The portrait of General Washington kneeling in the snow at Valley Forge is a poignant and moving testament to his Christianity.

Here is another example of political correctness gone awry. Many Christians are reluctant to use the word *Jew*, and many are prone to ask, "Are you Jewish?" It is perfectly proper to ask, if you really must know, "Are you a Jew?"

Yet a third example is in order. The hyphenated variety is the most overworked. When you hear a family name such as Costello, you may be tempted to ask, "Oh, are you Italian?" You are apt to get one of several replies such as, "Yeah," or "Yeah, I'm Italian-American." Other times, you might get, "No, I'm Irish as Paddy's pig." However, the most overworked are the hyphenated adjectives applied to members of the so-called minority races. The use of a hyphenated adjective does a disservice to all Americans. Assuming that an individual living in America is something less than American is belittling, unless that individual already belittles himself by proclaiming to be *African American* or *Mexican American* or *Indian American.*

From America's inception in the early seventeenth century, we have been assimilators. We have welcomed any and all who were of a similar mind—that is, to live free, free from a mandated religion, free to worship or not to worship, free to choose those who would carry on our affairs of government, free from tyranny, free to pursue our own individual destiny. This desire for freedom came with a price: you were expected to pull your own wagon, carry your own weight, and be self-sufficient.

Somewhere between then and now, America made an unwarranted and costly left turn. From my own observations and study, the execution of the left turn was begun during the administration of Woodrow Wilson. In his book *Woodrow Wilson and the Roots of Modern Liberalism*, Ronald J. Pestritto points out "[a] sharp departure from the traditional principles of American government, most notably the Constitution" from the synopsis found at The Barnes and Noble website.

Fringe elements and organizations, particularly those representing the Lesbian, Gay, Bisexual and Transsexual minority and those such as NAMBLA, The North American Man Boy Love Association have demanded that their sinful ways be taught to and practiced by the youth of America. Aberrant behavior is becoming the norm rather than the exception. Young men and women are forthright and seemingly proud of their unwed cohabitation, a status not considered something to brag about in this author's youth.

All the activities, practices, and other behaviors I perceive as problems to be addressed will be the subject of the final sections of this work. Gender inequality is an unacceptable condition and is the main thrust of this book.

Here and now I state with a copious amount of vehemence, "America's women have studiously and deliberately been denied their equal rights to be full partners in the governance and corporate management of The United States of America. For 405 years to be exact. This neglect is demeaning, cruel and wasteful!"

IT IS ABOUT TIME! AMERICA NEEDS A COMPETENT PRESIDENT

It is 5:00 p.m., Wednesday, September 29, 2010, as I begin my story. The first words are from CNSNews.com: "As New Fiscal Year Looms, Congress Has Passed 0 of 13 Appropriations Bills" required to keep this country of ours solvent. Does this disturbing announcement signal a catastrophic collapse of America? Is this the first time in our 223 years of existence that America may be unable to pay its bills? Unfortunately, this is not the first time.

For many years, we the people who make up these United States of America have saddled ourselves with a plethora of corrupt and inept employees, better known as politicians. We elected them. We called them president, representative, and senator. The majority have been the male of the species.

We have allowed ourselves to become their servants much to our chagrin. We have lost America. The beautiful and magnificent Lady Liberty stands tall and lovely in New York Harbor, yet no woman has stood tall, proud in the Oval Office. Meanwhile, males have stood proud and noticeably arrogant. The masters are being ruled by the servants; this is unacceptable!

How and when and by what means did this disaster have its genesis? This is an enigmatic question that I shall attempt to answer from the perspective of an amateur historian. This amateur is also an octogenarian who has had a lengthy love affair with America and has served her well and faithfully for the better part of a lifetime.

But let's start at the beginning and see if we can first ascertain from whence we came, how we conquered this land, and by whom it was accomplished. The final problem will be to propose attainable solutions in order to take back *our* United States of America. They belong to We the People, not to the politicians and the recipients of our social largesse.

Before there can be a reconquest of any continent, there must first be a conquest. Archeologists, paleontologists, and historians have debated, discussed, and argued about the identity or ethnicity the first peoples to take up residence in what is popularly known as the New World. Why the New World? Simply because North and South America were the last habitable continents to be settled by people from the other continents.

This story is about the **retaking, remaking and reshaping** of America, actually the United States of America. All else is peripheral to this central theme.

Who were the first to settle in, colonize, or lay claim to the area now identified as the forty-eight contiguous United States of America? In 1929, James Ridgley Whiteman discovered beautifully made flint points among mammoth bones in Blackwater Draw. The site is between Clovis and Portales, New Mexico. The artifacts from the site have been dated at 11,000 to 11,500 B.C..

The name given to the Paleo-Indian creators of the arrow and spear points was Clovis People, and sometimes the Llano People.[1]

More recently, archeologists have identified at least one site that predates Clovis. In his article from the Boston Globe, dated April 4, 2008, Colin Nickerson writes of David L. Jenkins, an archeologist from the University of Oregon who went digging in the Paisley Caves complex, on the coastline of present-day Oregon. He hit startling pay dirt. To be more exact, Jenkins found and identified fossilized human excrement called coprolites. Painstaking effort discovered human DNA dating back 14,300 years.[2]

With at least one Paleo-American doing his or her business in a cave in modern-day Oregon, I chose that as the point from which the conquest of America begins. The Paisley cave people may be the earliest yet dated; however, other scientists and interested amateur paleontologists, archeologists, and plain, old bone hunters keep turning up new sites.[3]

These new sites from Alaska's Bering Sea coastline to the southernmost reaches of South America oftentimes provide more questions than answers. For example, the Bering Sea land bridge, called Beringia, existed during several periods of the Pleistocene Ice Age. The present-day Bering Strait is now a shallow sea connecting another shallow sea, the Chukchi to the north and the shallow Bering Sea to the south. At various times, much water was concentrated in the ice caps, leaving the land bridge intact. All the evidence indicates that some Siberian peoples crossed this land bridge, which finally filled with water about fourteen thousand years ago.

There is ample evidence that some of these Siberian peoples eventually moved southward. Most moved south along the Pacific coast, unable to move eastward because of the persistent Canadian ice cap. Other peoples from Asia are believed to have used the Pacific coast shoreline or likely used watercraft to cross into North American landfalls.

For years, the Clovis people were considered the progenitors of Paleo-Indian life in North America, and the ancestors of the peoples of Central and South America. This is an ongoing search for the archeologists. For our story, we can stay right here in North America for now.

IN THE BEGINNING

Some fourteen thousand years ago, America was at the southernmost edge of the last continental ice sheet, Canada was almost entirely covered by glacial ice, while Alaska and eastern Siberia were almost free of glacial ice. A land bridge formed between Siberia and Alaska that permitted the mongoloid tribes of Siberia to migrate quite easily to the American continent. Along the western edge of the ice sheet, some areas became ice free or nearly so over time. These ice-free corridors permitted humans and animals to move southward to milder, more habitable climes.

As time passed, humans reached more habitable areas. Family groups expanded and intermingled with other immigrants. Cultures evolved into like-minded communities. As human populations grew, lack of edible materials forced some members to move on to greener pastures. These greener pastures included more game and more clean water. Some began cultivation of the soil for food and remained static for extended periods of time.

From the point of view of human archaeology, it falls in the Paleolithic and Mesolithic periods.

When the last episode of the Wisconsin glacial episode ended with what is known as the Tioga maxima, the glaciers began to retreat. Fertile soil was beneficial fallout. Canada had been totally covered by ice as had the Great Lakes area. Ice, in many places, had been as thick as a mile or more. As the glaciers melted, huge river gorges were formed and subsequently filled with melt water. Examples are the mighty Mississippi, the Ohio, the Missouri, the Erie, and the Hudson.

During the years between the terminus of the glacial advance and the dissolution of the great glaciers, the Paleo-Indians, identified variously as Native Americans or simply as Indians, increased, possibly by some 750 generations. Scholars have given estimates of pre-Columbian Native Americans at around ten to twelve million.[4] The big question still remains: Who were the first Europeans to explore this new world?

THE FIRST IMMIGRANTS

It is difficult, if not impossible, to state with any certainty who may have been the descendants of the Paisley Cave Llano people. Did they simply vanish? Did they intermarry with other immigrants, or did they maintain and expand their own culture? Archeologists are of the opinion that some indigenous peoples did indeed have a decipherable culture dating as far back as 5000 B.C. or 7000 B.C..

Quoted from *Wikipedia* to whom attribution is hereby made;

"5th millennium B.C. in North American history."

A Timeline

- 5000 B.C.: Early cultivation of food crops began in Mesoamerica

- 5000 B.C.: Native Americans in the Pacific Northwest from Alaska to California developed a fishing economy, with Salmon as a staple.

- 5000 B.C.: The Old Copper Culture of the Great Lakes area hammered the metal into various tools and ornaments such as knives, axes, awls, bracelets, rings and pendants

- Native Americans in the northern Great Lakes produced copper tools, ornaments, and utensils that they traded throughout the Great Plains and Ohio Valley.

- Shell ornaments and copper items at Indian Knoll in Kentucky provide evidence of an extensive trade system over several millennia.

- 4000 B.C.: Inhabitants of Mesoamerica cultivate maize (corn) while Peruvian natives cultivate beans and squash. Along the Mississippi River and its tributaries, the Native Americans engaged in commerce, planted crops, built ceremonial and burial mounds. Findings give testimony that they were of a religious nature, they also traded far and wide, as far as the Great Lakes or beyond.

The North American continent is large and presents a vast diversity of climate, flora, and fauna. It must have seemed like their own personal heaven to the hunter-gatherers and the neolithic agriculturists. Nevertheless, by the time the first Europeans arrived, no part of the continent north of Mexico had reached a stage that could be defined as civilization. In Mexico and on down into Central and South America, several highly developed cultures had evolved.

Between 1492 and 1620, the Indians were victims of the Spanish, who wanted to make the lands in and south of Mexico their own. The first North American Indians to be challenged were the pueblo of the southwest. Spaniards were challenging from the south via Mexico.

In the eastern part of the continent, the Iroquois and the Algonquians were challenged by English and

French colonists who were seeking wealth and new homes far from the strife in Europe. Now we know there existed North American Indians in the west, the southwest, up and down the Mississippi and its tributaries, and on the northeastern coast.

But the question is yet to be answered: How many tribes were there prior to 1620? Historians tell us that in 1891, the intrepid explorer, John Wesley Powell, leader of the first expedition down the Colorado River in 1869, provided us with the Map of the Linguistic Stocks of American Indians, Chiefly within the Present Limits of the United States. [5]

The map depicts the distribution of the fifty-eight Indian tribes based upon linguistic stock. Now that we have an overview of our continental beginnings, let us take another look backward to our Euro-Asiatic and our Judeo-Christian heritage.

THE BEGINNING OF CHRISTIANITY[6]

As we did with continental America, we need to go back in history to at least the birth of Jesus Christ, The exact date has never been determined. Historians, biblical scholars, antiquities students, and archeologists have proposed dates from 6 B.C. to A.D. 5. In order to have a solid understanding of timeframes and timelines, I will use B.C. to mean "before Christ" and A.D. will refer to the accepted meaning of "anno Domini" or "in the year of our Lord."

In this chapter, we must consider a much larger part of planet Earth. As a matter of fact, we must consider virtually all of the Middle East, Europe, and in some consequence, Africa and the major oceans and seas.

For millennia, the Israelites had awaited the coming of the Messiah. Modern Jewry still awaits this awesome event. At one point in time, Gabriel the Archangel announced to Mary, the virgin wife of Joseph, a Galilean carpenter, that she would become the mother of Jesus Christ the Son of God. Mary was instructed to name the Son of God Jesus, meaning "YHWH delivers." This, the Immaculate Conception, could well be considered the very beginning of Christianity. The Annunciation was made during the sixth month of Mary's cousin Elizabeth's pregnancy with her child, who would become known as John the Baptist.

The Christ Child was born in Bethlehem where Joseph and Mary had gone to pay their taxes. Little is known about the child Jesus until around the year A.D. 7, when Jesus astounded the religious leaders in the temple with his wisdom. A year or so later, the most dominate group of Pharisees, the School of Shammai, issued an edict that would later impact the mission of Jesus and the apostles. Bet or 'Beit' Shammai can mean both House of and School of in Hebrew but I chose to use 'School' because Shammai was a rabbinical figure, an opponent of Hillel, and had a Schul that taught his doctrine or vision of Judaism.

In the year A.D. 27, John the Baptist began his ministry; about two years later, Jesus began his ministry. John was beheaded by Herod in A.D. 29 but not before he had baptized Jesus. By about A.D. 30, Jesus was tried by Pilate, crucified on Calvary, and resurrected.

In A.D. 33, the Shammai expelled all non-Hebrew Jews from Jerusalem, and the followers of the apostles of Jesus, the Christians, were caught up in the turmoil and scattered far and wide. Before undergoing his conversion, Paul of Tarsus persecuted the Christians. Later, he returned to Jerusalem where he boldly proclaimed Christ. This enraged the elders, and Paul was forced to go back to his hometown of Tarsus, a Mediterranean coastal city in southern Turkey. Mollified, the elders thus permitted the church to rest. Shortly thereafter, Peter founded the church in Antioch.

In A.D. 44, James, the brother of John, was beheaded; the term *Christian* replaced *believers* to identify the followers of Christ. It is believed that the book of

Galatians and the book of James were written around A.D. 46–48. In A.D. 49, the Council of Jerusalem met to discuss Gentiles in the church. James issued a decree that Gentiles are no longer required to follow the Torah and are not obligated to be circumcised.

The Virgin Mary died in A.D. 52, at Ephesus, aged sixty-four (this date and age are questionable though). The Catholic Church maintains that Mary was immediately resurrected and assumed into heaven. They commemorate this event on the Feast of the Assumption. In this same timeframe, two more books of the Bible are believed to have been written, the 1 Thessalonians and 2 Thessalonians as well as the book of Matthew in Aramaic. The book of Mark had been previously written probably in Aramaic and translated into Greek. Matthew was also translated into Greek later on.

Three more books of the Bible are believed to have been written between A.D. 53 and A.D. 54, the book of Romans and 1 Corinthians and 2 Corinthians. Between A.D. 60 and A.D. 63, the Gospel of Luke, Colossians, and Ephesians were written. Several more books of the Bible were written before A.D. 67, when Peter and Paul were martyred by Nero. Mark was also martyred during this same period. A full rebellion began against Rome when Simeon led the Jewish Christians out of Jerusalem in the year 81.

The Renaissance c. 1400 – c. 1600. breathed new life into Europe. "The Renaissance may be considered as a sort of a bridge between the Middle Ages and the Modern Age." Social, economic, and political changes were hallmarks of the age. The Italian Renaissance of the fifteenth century continued the artistic and literary tradition. The Middle Ages was a period from the 5th to 16th centuries. The Renaissance was the period between the 14th and the 16th centuries.

Social, economic, and political changes were hallmarks of the age. The Italian Renaissance of the fifteenth century continued the artistic and literary tradition. The Middle Ages was a period from the 5th to 16th centuries. The Renaissance was the period between the 14th and the 16th centuries.

Towns and cities sprang up, and the Hanseatic League was formed in Northern Europe in 1158. Many cities in the Holy Roman Empire became members, as did London. Germans began colonizing Eastern Europe, which was outside the Holy Roman Empire.

While the Portuguese and Spanish mariners were opening up trade routes worldwide during the sixteenth century, they also colonized large areas of the New World. Spain opened up the Pacific trade routes between Asia and the Americas. Not to be outdone, the mariners of Portugal became the masters of the Indian Ocean trade.

THE PROTESTANT REFORMATION[9]

In 1517, Martin Luther published "The Ninety-Five Theses," which was the beginning of the Protestant Reformation. The Reformation was also called the Protestant revolt. It made Protestantism the first of the non-Catholic Christian belief systems; the religious war lasted for over 130 years and ended with the Treaty of Westphalia.

In terms of everyday life, what did these changes do for the common people? What happened to the tillers of the soil, the small craft shops, the seafarers, and the scholars?

Let's take a step back and look at some of the events that preceded the Protestant revolt. Most of the known civilized world was included in the Roman Empire. Roman emperors exercised secular rule over the people. The Catholic Church was the only organized religion, and the pope was as influential as or more so than the emperors.

In order for us to establish the beginnings of those who would later become the founders of America, we must take a very quick look back to the year A.D. 300. In that year, there were some sixty million people in the Roman Empire, about fifteen million of whom were Christians. After having survived the empire-wide persecutions ordered by the emperor Decius, the Christians were scattered throughout the empire. [7]

Diocletian was then the emperor and in A.D. 303, also ordered a general persecution of the Christians. Constantine became emperor in A.D. 312 and, by the edict of Milano, ended the persecutions. Constantine recognized the Christian Church in A.D. 312.

Wars continued off and on for the next seven hundred or so years, until the patriarch of Constantinople (the pope of the Eastern or Byzantine church) and the pope in Rome excommunicated each other in what became known as the great schism.

The next act of major consequence to the Christian community was when Emperor Leo III introduced Christian principles into law when he issued the Ecloga. Finally in A.D. 380, Theodosius I proclaimed Christianity to be the sole religion of the Roman Empire.

The empire was not recognized as holy until A.D. 962 when Otto I was crowned king of Germany. The term *holy* first came into use in A.D. 1157 under the reign of Frederick I Barbarossa.

All the while the Roman Empire was having its troubles, Islam was making gains in the east. They attempted to capture Constantinople in A.D. 677 but failed. Just ten years later, a Merovingian ruler, Pepin, united the Frankish territories. He was succeeded by his son, Charles Martel, who formed an alliance with the church, which then aided the Merovingian dynasty and also helped Christianity to expand into Germany.

In A.D. 700, the Benedictine missionaries completed the work begun by St. Gregory the Great, and all England was converted to Christianity. By A.D. 735, Venerable Bede, an Anglo-Saxon Benedictine scholar, had written—in Latin—his seminal work, *History of the English Church and People.*

In A.D. 715, the epic poem "Beowulf" was written in Old English. The author remains anonymous to this day, but the poem is certainly Christian in nature as it exemplifies early medieval society in England and shows roots in Old Testament law.

Schools were established during another renaissance under the rule of Charlemagne and the direct supervision of an Anglo-Saxon Benedictine, Alcuin. Charlemagne was crowned emperor on Christmas Day A.D. 800 by the pope in Rome.

Charlemagne died in A.D. 814 without leaving any competent successors. During this chaotic period, the empire was invaded by, among others, the Muslims. The great empire of Charlemagne fell apart, not to rise again until Otto the Great became emperor in A.D. 962.

Meanwhile, across the channel in England, King Alfred the Great constructed a system of government and education, codified English law, and, in various ways, furthered the national culture. Fortunately, Alfred assured competent succession, and when he died in A.D. 899, his good works were continued.

Excesses and poor leadership within the Catholic Church—highlighted by selecting an eighteen-year-old as Pope John XII in A.D. 955—caused a lessening of respect and no little cause for concern within the ecclesiastical leadership.

PURITANS AND PILGRIMS[10]

Let us begin with the Puritans: just who were they, and what defined them? The Puritans were a part of the Protestant Reformation begun by Martin Luther. Their religious leanings were toward the Calvinistic, quite rigid and theocratic. When Elizabeth I became queen in 1559, she entered into compromises and agreements with the Anglican Church. These did not sit too well with the Baptists and Presbyterians.

These denominations felt the Church of England had not gone far enough in ridding itself of the papist ritual, its corrupt practices, and dogma. The Puritans wanted more purification of the church as preached by John Calvin. They sought a more complete reformation of both the religious and the secular life.

The Presbyterian branch of the Puritan Party was ultimately defeated in Parliament. Soon after the suppression of nonconformist ministers in 1583, a minority attempted to separate from the church. They ultimately sought refuge in the religion-tolerant Netherlands in 1608. This group was later to be identified as Pilgrims, meaning "wanderers." They were from then on apolitical.

On the other hand, their brethren, the Puritans, were really just as religious, but were more willing to compromise in order to participate in the secular portion of their lives. The Puritans were a force to be reckoned with in sixteenth- and seventeenth-century

Europe. When Queen Elizabeth—the last of the Tudors—died childless in 1603, she was succeeded by King James I, the son of Mary, Queen of Scots.

Prior to his ascendancy to the throne, James had written his belief in the divine right of kings; in *The True Law of Free Monarchies*. James was a devout Protestant and believed—for biblical reasons—kings were higher beings than other men. King James was not looked upon favorably by his subjects. He was considered untrustworthy and crude. He did not care for the Puritans and noted that "I will make them conform or I will harry them out of the land."

The most obvious threat to King James was not the Puritans but Catholic Spain, which was a threat to both. The inquisition was ruthless, and non-Catholics were hunted down, jailed, tortured on the rack, and executed for their heretical anti-Catholic beliefs and practices. During James's first year on the throne, English troops defeated Spain, and thus ended the inquisition.

The Pilgrims, meanwhile, became subject to stresses, which come to all who are visitors in a foreign land. Plus, the threat of the inquisition was ever present. In the end, the Pilgrims decided to return to England and make preparations to go to the New World.

After many delays, thirty-five Pilgrim and Puritans under William Bradford and sixty-seven skilled workmen and indentured servants departed Plymouth on September 6, 1620, aboard the *Mayflower*. They were bound for Virginia, where they planned to start a colony. They had intended to charter another ship, the *Speedwell*, which, after two attempts, was declared not seaworthy. This resulted in several Pilgrims—including their beloved Pastor Robinson—being left behind to await the return of the *Mayflower* and a second crossing.

The *Mayflower*—which was actually a cargo ship—was really overcrowded and had no staterooms, toilets, or other amenities. The weather was uncooperative; it was and still is the typhoon season in the Atlantic. The weather at times forced the ship to heave to, meaning to face into the wind resulting in little or no forward progress. As a result, most, if not all, the passengers suffered from seasickness and other discomforts. Despite horrendous conditions and poor navigation, the *Mayflower* made landfall sixty-six days later. She was six hundred miles off course when the anchor was dropped at Cape Cod, near present-day Provincetown, Massachusetts.

William Bradford, a prominent member of the Pilgrim travelers, kept a journal of the voyage. He recorded that only one passenger, a young man, died just as the ship was nearing the coast. It is interesting to note here that during one storm, a passenger named John Howland came above deck and was swept overboard. Howland managed to grab hold of the topsail halyards and was rescued. This augured well for some of his latter-day American ancestors: presidents Franklin Roosevelt and George Bush, actor Humphrey Bogart, and founder of the Mormons, Joseph Smith.

After some deliberation among passengers and the ship's captain, a decision was made to attempt to locate a suitable place for habitation along Hudson River. Turbulent seas, however, nearly wrecked them on some shoals off Cape Cod. This near-disaster caused them to hastily change their minds and return to their safe anchorage off Provincetown in Cape Cod Bay, some distance from the northern portion of the Virginia colony for which they had permission to colonize. This occurred on November 11, 1620.

After their near-disastrous foray south to find a settlement site near Hudson River, the northern edge of the Virginia Grant, the *Mayflower* headed back to the shelter of Cape Cod. There was evidence of very troubling dissatisfaction among the passengers. Several of the passengers had paid their passage by becoming indentured servants to the paying Pilgrims.

After some deliberation among passengers and the ship's captain, a decision was made to attempt to locate a suitable place for habitation along Hudson River. Turbulent seas, however, nearly wrecked them on some shoals off Cape Cod.

THE *MAYFLOWER* COMPACT[11]

Quoting William Bradford, "Being thus arrived in a good harbor and brought safe to land, they fell upon their knees and blessed the God of heaven, who had brought them over the vast and furious ocean and delivered them from all the perils thereof."

There was evidence of very troubling dissatisfaction among the passengers. Several of the passengers had paid their passage by becoming indentured servants to the paying Pilgrims.

It was readily apparent to the Pilgrims that they were in need of some formal leadership. To that end, the men—both Pilgrim and Puritan, several of whom were the indentured servants—put together a document of governance.

The *Mayflower* compact—inspired by the aforementioned pastor, John Robinson—was that document. Since it is quite short, it is quoted here in full:

> In the name of God, Amen. We, whose names are underwritten, the Loyal Subjects of our dread Sovereign Lord, King James, by the Grace of God, of England, France and Ireland, King, Defender of the Faith, e&. Having undertaken for the Glory of God, and Advancement of the Christian Faith, and the Honour of our King and Country, a voyage to plant the first colony in the northern parts of Virginia; do by these presents, solemnly and mutually

in the Presence of God and one of another, covenant and combine ourselves together into a civil Body Politick, for our better Ordering and Preservation, and Furtherance of the Ends aforesaid; And by Virtue hereof to enact, constitute, and frame, such just and equal Laws, Ordinances, Acts, Constitutions and Offices, from time to time, as shall be thought most meet and convenient for the General good of the Colony; unto which we promise all due submission and obedience. In Witness whereof we have hereunto subscribed our names at Cape Cod the eleventh of November, in the Reign of our Sovereign Lord, King James of England, France and Ireland, the eighteenth, and of Scotland the fifty-fourth. Anno Domini, 1620.

THE LIFE AND TIMES OF
THE PILGRIMS [12] [13]

Life was excruciatingly difficult for the Pilgrims. Food was always in short supply, disease was ever present, and the climate during the winters was brutal. The Pilgrims were devout in their trust in the power and will of God. They accepted their fate as God's children; for them, traveling to a distant land and settling here was preordained.

The daily life of these good people was largely devoted to small plot farming, fishing, and hunting for game. They raised pumpkin, squash, beans, lettuce, and corn. According to a blog by Eric Berger in the *Houston Chronicle*, dated November 24, 2005, he noted that the History Channel and food historians provided a list of the likely foods on the menu of the first Thanksgiving celebrated by the Pilgrims and their Wampanoag friends in 1621.

They feasted for three days on the following:

- Seafood: eel, clams, fish, and lobster
- Wild fowl: turkey, goose, duck, crane, swan, partridge, and eagles
- Dried currants, parsnips
- Meat: venison and seal
- Grain: wheat flour and Indian corn

- Vegetables: pumpkin, peas, beans, onions, lettuce, radishes, and carrots
- Fruit: plums and grapes
- Nuts: walnuts, chestnuts, and acorns
- Herbs and seasonings: olive oil, liverwort, leeks

The daily life of the Pilgrims was far different from that bountiful first Thanksgiving. The Pilgrims have usually been shown as wearing only black and white. Actually, they favored casual, daily wear—browns, greens, even maroons, and other dark colors. Black and white clothing was reserved for the Sabbath or other special occasions. Men wore a traditional hat, breeches, a collarless shirt, and no belt. Children, both boys and girls up until around age eight, wore a dress-like gown. Clothes were made of wool and linen. The wealthier pilgrims wore cotton clothing.

Children were not allowed to sit during meals, nor were they allowed to speak. The meal for the Sabbath was baked beans prepared with molasses and a piece of salt pork. The preparation of the beans began on Saturday night, cooking all night in a bake pot in front of the fireplace.

Schooling was done by parents. really home schooling.

The government of the colony was vested in a governor and seven assistants. This governing group met every March and made or revised the laws under which the Pilgrims conducted their daily lives. The governor and his assistants were selected by the General Court, which consisted of colony members. There was also a Grand Jury, the highest standing organization in the colony. This jury decided the penalty for crimes.

Taxes (called rates) were paid by every man based upon the English pound but generally paid in Indian wheat. Married women were not allowed to own land, goods, or hold positions of authority. Single women and widows had some of these rights, and widows were often called upon for advice.

When the Pilgrims first arrived, they lived in dugouts or tents. They quickly learned how to build huts. Later on, the Swedish settlers taught them how to build log cabins.

Up to this point, we have learned that our Pilgrim-Puritan forefathers were hardy, they were Protestants, they believed in themselves as capable of governing their lives and managing the affairs of government in a particular, novel fashion: democratic.

Who were those responsible for shaping the character of their fellow Pilgrims and that of the new colonies? First, we might look toward their most beloved pastor, John Robinson. Pastor Robinson was among the first separatists. He was the spiritual guide for the Pilgrims during their stay in Holland. Pastor Robinson, also known as the Apostle of Leyden, became ill and died in late February 1625, never having joined his flock in their newfound paradise.

William Bradford, a most godly and learned man, kept a journal of this first Puritan-Pilgrim colony. Bradford was the most logical choice to succeed John Carver as governor, when Carver died quite suddenly in 1621. Below is a quotation from Bradford's *Of*

Plymouth Plantation, which he completed around 1650 after having been governor for some thirty years. [14]

PRIVATE AND COMMUNAL FARMING (1623)

All this while no supply was heard of, neither knew they when they might expect any. So they began to think how they might raise as much corn as they could, and obtain a better crop than they had done, that they might not still thus languish in misery. [At length, after much debate of things, the governor (with the advice of the chiefest among them) gave way that they should set corn every man for his own particular and, in that regard, trust to themselves, in all other thing, to go on in the general way as before.]

And so assigned to every family a parcel of land, according to the proportion of their number, for that end, only for present use (but made no division for inheritance) and ranged all boys and youth under some family. This had very good success, for it made all hands very industrious, so as much more corn was planted than otherwise would have been by any means the Governor or any other could use, and saved him a great deal of trouble, and gave far better content. [The women now went willingly into the field and took their little ones with them to set corn, which before would allege weakness and inability, whom to have compelled would have been thought great tyranny and oppression.]

The experience that was had in this common course and condition, tried sundry years and that amongst godly and sober men [may well evince the vanity of that conceit of Plato's and other ancients applauded by some of later times; and that the taking away of property and bringing in community into a commonwealth would make them happy and flourishing, as if they were wiser than God. For this community (so far as it was) was found to breed much confusion and discontent and retard much employment that would have been to their benefit and comfort.]

For the young men, that were most able and fit for labor and service, did repine that they should spend their time and strength to work for other men's wives and children without any recompense. The strong, or man of parts, had no more in division of victuals and clothes than he that was weak and not able to do a quarter the other could; this was thought injustice.

The aged and graver men to be ranked and equalized in labors and victuals, clothes etc., with the meaner and younger sort, thought it some indignity and disrespect unto them. [And for men's wives to be commanded to do service for other men, as dressing their meat, washing their clothes, etc., they deemed it a kind of slavery] neither could many husbands well brook it.

Upon the point all being to have alike, and all to do alike, they thought themselves in the like condition, and one as good as another; and so, if it did not cut off those relations that

God hath set amongst men, yet it did at least much diminish and take off the mutual respects that should be preserved amongst them. And would have been worse if they had been men of another condition. Let none object this is men's corruption, and nothing to the course itself. I answer, seeing all men have this corruption in them, God in His wisdom saw another course fitter for them. [14]

It must be noted that, as godly and as cooperative as the Puritans professed to be, there was dissention within their democratic situation. Not unlike this twenty-first century.

COLONIAL COALESCENCE, GRIEVANCE, GOVERNANCE

By the year 1700, the Anglo population of the future United States had reached 275,000; Boston, the largest city, had a population of 7,000; and New York City, the second largest, at 5,000. The Protestant governments began to express their dominance, first in Massachusetts when in 1700, all Roman Catholics priests were ordered to leave the colony within three months under penalty of life imprisonment or execution. Shortly thereafter, New York passed a similar law. [15]

The North American continent was by no means all Anglo. The French established a settlement in Detroit in 1701, and in New Orleans in 1718. The northern colonies were Protestant Pilgrims. Farther south, however, in the Maryland Colony, the Anglican church was the religion of choice and became the official church in 1702, financially supported by taxation of all free men, male servants, and slaves.

South Carolina followed this precedent and adopted the Anglican religion as the state religion in November 1706.

Slavery—though a vile custom and not worthy of humanity—had a huge impact on America. I will not, however, attempt to deal with that subject in this work other than to note at different points any facts pertinent to the work and the time frame at which they occur.

I must take note at this point, the first of our Founding Fathers, Benjamin Franklin, was born in Boston on January 17, 1706. In 1729, he began publishing the *Pennsylvania Gazette*, which eventually became the most popular colonial newspaper.

By the year 1720, the population of the colonies had exploded to 475,000. Boston held on to its first rank position at 12,000, followed by the rapidly expanding Philadelphia at 10,000, and then New York at 7,000.

Tea was introduced into the colonies in 1714, the same year King George I ascended the throne. In retrospect, every American realized that trouble was brewing along with the tea, and the taxes on those little green leaves were quickly increasing. That tempest in a teapot was just over the horizon.

By the year 1760, the population of the colonies had reached 1,500,000, Boston was virtually destroyed by a raging fire, and King George III ascended the English throne. The colonists, who had been pretty self-reliant for one hundred and forty years, were very independent and strong-willed. The British Parliament passed the Stamp Act in 1765, on top of the Sugar Act of 1764, plus other repressive and oppressive acts. Some merchants and tradesmen then formed the Sons of Liberty to protest the Stamp Act.

The enraged colonists created the Stamp Act Congress, which delivered its answer to the Crown. In its response to this hostile act by the colonials, Britain repealed the Stamp Act, but immediately passed the Declaratory Act, which said that Great Britain was "superior (and boss of) the American colonies "in all cases whatsoever."[16]

The colonials were jubilant that they had forced the repeal of the hated Stamp Act. However, few took notice of the Declaratory Act. One who did was John Adams, who wondered if Parliament would "lay a tax in consequence of it." He got his answer in the Townshend Revenue Act of 1767, which was designed to raise 40,000 pounds per year to administer the colonies. It was a most repressive tax and was certain to further anger the colonists who rightfully resented "taxation without representation."[17]

Rebellion was on the near horizon. The Townshend Act caused as much or more resentment among the colonists that in 1768, when a sloop owned by John Hancock was impounded for violations of Trade Regulations, crowds of Bostonians mobbed the customs house, forcing the officials to flee to a British warship in the harbor.

Troops from England and Nova Scotia marched in to occupy Boston on October 1, 1768. The Bostonians offered no resistance; they simply changed tactics and refused to buy British goods. Trade dried up and the powerful merchants of Britain interceded on behalf of the colonials. This was only a temporary stopgap. British monarchs, as they had a tendency to do, failed to realize the anger of the colonists was righteous and continued their dictatorial practices. On March 5, 1770, a mob of Bostonians began throwing snowballs, stones, and sticks at a British sentinel. A British officer,

Captain Thomas Preston, called in additional troops who were also attacked.

The soldiers fired into the mob killing three on the spot. One, Crispus Attucks, an American slave, merchant seaman and dockworker of Wampanoag and African descent was the first casualty of the impending Revolutionary War for Independence. Also killed were Samuel Gray, a ropemaker; and James Caldwell, a mariner. Eight others were wounded, two of whom later died of their wounds.

The massacre was the event that led directly to the Revolutionary War. This book is not intended as a study of the war. Rather, it seeks some answers to the problems that have since arisen.

POSTWAR GOVERNANCE

The Thirteen Colonies organized the First Continental Congress in 1774. They met in Carpenter's Hall in Philadelphia from September 5 to October 26. There were several different governing bodies during the war. They were the model for the governments shortly after the war and until the Constitution was finally written and passed by Congress on September 17, 1787, and ratified on June 21, 1788, when the ninth state, New Hampshire, ratified the Constitution.

On December 15, 1791, Virginia ratified the Bill of Rights and that most desirable of freedoms finally locked into place. The Puritan/Pilgrims—God bless them all—had the foresight and perseverance to begin the foundation of mankind's greatest achievement, to worship our Holy Redeemer as we choose. That privilege shall be ours until we fail to protect it. God Bless America! Let us preserve her and the values upon which she was founded.

Obviously, God had great things in mind for this newborn nation. George Washington was sent to guide this neophyte but God-loving nation through her pre-natal ordeals and her first creeping and crawling until she could stand tall and call out to those seeking refuge, "Come, come all are welcome here; accept us for who and what we are, attempt not to deprive us of our Christian virtues so costly attained and fondly cherished."

General and President George Washington epitomized nobility in its highest sense. An unselfish leader, one who saw his duty performed superbly, and stepped down from office, and into America's brilliant history. President Washington had the wisdom and faith to decline further presidential service. He was wise enough to recognize one man could give only so much without taking too much. He set the term limit for presidential service. He earned his rest. Franklin Roosevelt should have been nearly so wise. Arrogance, narcissism, and despotism were his chief attributes, leaving intelligence, brilliance, and leadership a waste.

The tenor of leadership was set by our first six presidents. With only a few exceptions, it has been all downhill thereafter.

MAKING THE SAME MISTAKES

THE PLAYERS AND THEIR ACTIONS

I fail to understand the mentality of this great nation's political movers and shakers. We have been cursed by having far too many incompetent members of Congress, 535 in total, who are supposed to be a co-equal body with the executive and with the judiciary. Far too often, the executive branch seizes power by the use of questionable actions. Executive orders were never intended as a substitute for adequate legislation, nor are signing statements that usually serve to negate the very purpose of, or portions of, the legislation to which it becomes a part. Lies, deception, duplicity, and power plays have served this country badly.

After rereading the first sentence, I have reminded myself: power for the sake of power is the mentality. Power driven by greed and a total absence of honor or sense of shame has led us down this torturous path. I should like to make a case for a substantial portion of our troubles. Party (factional) loyalty was not a real problem during the terms of our first six presidents. Beginning with Andrew Jackson, the first Democrat president, arrogance, pride and power, coupled with the spoils system became the de facto way of doing government business.

Very little has changed throughout the administrations of the succeeding thirty-eight administrations. The most egregious crimes have been committed by presidents loyal to, and sycophantic of, the Democratic Party. The worst offender was by far, Woodrow Wilson, our twenty-eighth—and likely, first treasonous—president. No one kept track of his behavior nor was he vetted thoroughly.

Wilson, while a professor at Princeton University carried on an extra-marital affair with the wife of one of his colleagues, a Professor Peck, earning for Wilson the sobriquet Peck's Bad Boy. He was stupid enough to write letters to her making promises he never kept. Wilson's reputation did not escape the attention of high-ranking members of the Zionist movement in New York City. They needed a patsy to carry out their plans to gain control of Palestine as the permanent home for the world's displaced Jews.

President Taft did not respond favorably to demands of the Zionist movement to abrogate the most-favored-nation treaty with Tsarist Russia, a Christian nation despised by the Zionists. Jacob Schiff (reportedly the Illuminati Jewish Banker who had the clout to and supposedly did order the elimination of Czar Nichols and his entire family) and his associates, all Zionists, planned to get rid of Taft. They financed and formed the Bull Moose Party and persuaded Theodore Roosevelt to run in order to bleed off votes from Taft. Wilson won, while polling only 42 percent of the popular vote.

> With their man now in the White House (a man of compromised morals), the Zionist plan for a central bank; renewed legislation for an income tax–(abolished in 1872 after it had

been employed to finance the Civil War); and American involvement in a global war, was a fait accompli. [18]

One of Wilson's first acts was, without mentioning "central", establishing the Federal Reserve Bank. "On June 23, 1913, Wilson initiated a special session of the Sixty-Third Congress to vote on the "Federal Reserve Act," a piece of legislation bought and paid for by Zionist intrigues. It was on December 19, 1913, that Wilson pushed the bill through the Senate while most members were home for Christmas. [19]

> Operating as agents for "Lord" Nathaniel Rothschild, the monetary resources of America were now in the hands of three Jews: Jacob Schiff of Kuhn, Loeb Bank; Paul Warburg, appointed by Wilson as the Fed's first chairman; and George Blumenthal, a high official of JPMorgan Chase & Co. Henceforth, the "treasury" of the United States would forever be in the hands of the Jews. Ibid

It is ludicrous to accept that Wilson's shoddy conduct had escaped the notice of every member of the New Jersey government. He later served as governor of New Jersey; and juicy scandals are the mainstay of politics in New Jersey. [20][21]

Wilson actually had at least two affairs with other women, later marrying one of them. The affair with the wife of his Princeton neighbor led directly to America's involvement in World War I. For this alone, Wilson could well have been charged with and found guilty of treason. [22]

Samuel Untermeyer of one of New York City's most successful and extremely wealthy law firms presented at President Wilson's Oval Office. Mr. Untermeyer produced a packet of letters for Wilson's examination. Wilson acknowledged them as written by him to Mrs. Peck. Untermeyer informed President Wilson that Mrs. Peck was suing Wilson for $40,000 in exchange for the letters and her silence. Stunned, Wilson told Untermeyer that he was not able to pay such an enormous amount.

Mr. Untermeyer suggested that Wilson give it some thought and that he would return in a few days. When Untermeyer returned a few days later, Wilson reiterated that he could not afford $40,000. *The trap was sprung!* Untermeyer told Wilson that he would pay the money from his own pocket in exchange for Wilson's promise to appoint to the Supreme Court a Zionist Jew, Louis Debnitz Brandeis, as soon as a seat became vacant. Wilson readily agreed and on June 5, 1916, he appointed Brandeis to the Court. [23] [24] [25]

What political machinations transpired to force Wilson to ask for a declaration of war even though he was elected to a second term vowing that no American would set foot on European soil? It all came together with the establishment of the Federal Reserve Bank. This was simply a Jewish banking consortium with no reserves. They printed money with no hard currency backing and made interest bearing loans from their

Federal Reserve Bank to the American government. This was the conduit to pay off the Zionist loan sharks.

Concurrently, Wilson's Sixteenth amendment served to reduce these tax-paying Americans to near servitude. The Amendment further served to establish the IRS as a division of the Treasury Department.

The precise act of taking America into the European conflict was a bold-faced lie to an unwary and never vigilant Wilson. Justice Brandeis volunteered his opinion to President Wilson that the sinking of the SS *Sussex* by a German submarine in the English Channel—with the loss of lives of United States citizens—justified the declaration of war against Germany by the United States.

Relying entirely upon the legal opinion and untruthful declaration of Justice Brandeis, President Wilson—without verifying the word of Justice Brandeis—addressed both houses of Congress on April 2, 1917. He appealed to Congress to declare war against Germany, and they did on April 7, 1917.[27]

There were just a couple of little problems. For one, no SS *Sussex* was sunk with the loss of American lives, and apparently, not a single member of Congress sought to validate that one deciding factor which may have kept us out of a costly foreign war.[27] If, in fact, the information presented is true, Wilson was a careless and ruthless custodian of the office of the presidency. Had all the facts been available at the time, Wilson would have been a prime candidate for impeachment, a trial for treason, and ultimately execution.

NOTE: The White House webpage fails to acknowledge any of the foregoing. Wilson is there portrayed as a champion of Americans. Obama has had the entire site redone favorable to Democrats.

Following the war, Wilson went to Europe to pitch his idea for a "league of nations." When he returned to Washington to present the Treaty of Versailles to the Senate, the winds of fortune had turned against him. His pleading rhetoric, "Dare we reject it and break the heart of the world?" fell upon deaf ears. The Republicans were by then in control. The treaty was defeated by seven votes. The United States never became a member of the League. Wilson subsequently suffered a stroke and died in 1924.

Wilson's ignoble legacies—the Federal Reserve, income tax, the IRS, and the graves of some 940,000 gallant American dead from WW I—remain to this day.

Thirty-one Republicans signed a manifesto assuring voters that a vote for Warren G. Harding in the presidential election of 1920 was a vote for the League of Nations. Unfortunately, Harding didn't see it that way. He saw it as a mandate to stay out of the League. He was elected, garnering 60 percent of the popular vote, beating the Democratic contenders Governor James Cox of Ohio and Franklin Delano Roosevelt of New York.

A favorable Congress insured Harding's ability to pass legislation he had promised. The Congress got Harding's signature on bills eliminating wartime controls, slashing taxes, establishing a federal budget system, restoring a high protective tariff, and imposing tight limitations on immigration. Harding was carrying out his campaign promise of "less government in business and more business in government." Even the normally liberal press hailed Harding as a wise statesman.

All was not smooth sailing though in the Harding administration. Word reached Harding that some in his administration were using their position for personal enrichment. Beginning to sound all too familiar, is it not?

In the summer of 1923, President Harding decided to take a trip out west accompanied by his secretary of commerce, Herbert Hoover. Mr. Harding asked Hoover, "Would you, for the good of the country and the party, expose it publicly or would you bury it?" Hoover was in favor of publishing it, Harding demurred fearing the political repercussions. It would have made no difference; Harding died in San Francisco of a heart attack in August.

At 2:30 in the morning on August 3, 1923, Vice President Calvin Coolidge learned that he was president of the United States. His father, a notary public, administered the oath of office while Coolidge had his hand on the family Bible. Coolidge was a staunch conservative, honest, and trustworthy. He had inherited a mess in Washington and set about cleaning house. He refused to use federal power to check the growing boom nor did he intervene to support the depressed agricultural economy. His first message to Congress in December of 1923 called for isolation in foreign policy, and for tax cuts, economy, and limited aid to farmers.

Coolidge became very popular and, in 1924, he garnered more than 54 percent of the popular vote. In his inaugural, Coolidge noted that the country had reached a seldom-seen sense of contentment and pledged to maintain the status quo. The genius of President Coolidge, as Walter Lippmann pointed out in 1926, was his talent for effectively doing nothing: "This active inactivity suits the mood and certain of the needs of the country admirably. It suits all the business interests which want to be let alone... And it suits all those who have become convinced that government in this country has become dangerously complicated and top-heavy..."[28]

Coolidge was well-known for being a man of few words. One story reports that a lady said to President Coolidge, "I am told that you cannot be coaxed to respond with more than two words; I will bet that I can get you to speak more than two words."

Coolidge responded, "You lose." He was not called Silent Cal for no reason.

In 1928, Hoover became the Republican nominee. It is hard to imagine a man better equipped for the job. Born to a Quaker blacksmith in a small Iowa village, he enrolled in Stanford University when it opened and graduated as a mining engineer. He married his college sweetheart and they headed for China where Hoover, working for a private corporation, became China's leading engineer at age twenty-six. Hoover spent much of his life as an administrator in civil service endeavors, helping the poor, starving, and homeless.

Luck was not to be on Hoover's side. No sooner had he been elected that the stock market crashed and the Great Depression began. The notion that the Great Depression was Hoover's fault is ludicrous. Regardless, the Democrats made a point of laying the blame on Hoover, and Franklin Roosevelt—who knew better—shamelessly rode that theme all the way to the White House in 1932.

Thus began one of the most ballyhooed presidential administrations in our history. There are few reliable criteria by which we can measure the baseness of the Wilson administration versus that of Roosevelt's. Both men were narcissistic, arrogant demagogues. Not unlike the forty-fourth president who followed Roosevelt seventy-six years later, both made promises they could not or would not keep. Many of Roosevelt's New Deal components were declared unconstitutional, and rather than demanding the Democratic Congress to do a better job of legislative preparation, Roosevelt—not unlike Obama—laid the blame on the Supreme Court.

Roosevelt was so haughty that—rather than getting decent legislation from a willing Congress onto his desk—he blamed the mess on Hoover and wasted time that may have been better used to slow the Great Depression. Sure does have a ring of "I have heard this before," does it not?

To make matters worse, Roosevelt won handily in 1936. FDR—in the first of his regular fireside chats following his second inaugural and speaking in his grandiose, flamboyant, and haughty style—did the unthinkable. He proposed that he would have Congress prepare legislation to alter the size of the Supreme Court. His proposal would add one new associate justice for every sitting justice aged seventy or older because they were having trouble handling the caseload. A study proved that to be an outright lie. The Court was up-to-date and had no problems or backlogs.

This attempt by Roosevelt was an attempt to permanently alter the balance of power among the three constitutional branches and effectively allow the executive to become a monarch. Fortunately, for America, and unfortunately, for the majority leader of the Senate, Senator Joe Robinson of Arkansas, a heat wave swept over Washington in the summer of 1937. FDR had the unmitigated gall to "order" the majority leader to get the necessary legislation passed.

One Democratic senator from Montana, Burton K. Wheeler, a fellow progressive and ally of Robert M. La Follette, and La Follette's running mate in 1924, confronted the tiger in his lair. Wheeler told Roosevelt in very forceful terms, "I will *not* support your scheme to change the Supreme Court." Roosevelt was furious that any Democrat would have the temerity to defy him in one of his most critical moments.[29]

The opposition to the deceptively titled Judicial Procedures Reform Bill of 1937—but better and more properly known as the court-packing scheme—was fierce. The pressure and the heat wave took their toll on a valiant Joe Robinson; he had a heart attack and died. The court-packing scheme died with Robinson and FDR never had a "Do as I say" court. Roosevelt spent his prodigious skills and his political capital poorly. History notes that America would likely have shed the shackles of the Great Depression rather than having to depend on a wartime economy to bring about prosperity.

Franklin Roosevelt like Wilson had numerous very public faults. Those who loved him adored him, many never knew or would believe FDR was at best a to-the-manor-born aristocratic bully; at worst, a wealthy, power-hungry, autocrat. The rest, knowing him for what he was and did, loathed him.

At this writing, FDR is our third-highest-rated president. History will likely present a far less lovable and more thoroughly researched and evaluated history of this unethical, unfaithful, despicable showoff.

Franklin Roosevelt's death early in his fourth term dropped the burden of the presidency onto the sturdy shoulders of Harry S. Truman, a World War I Captain of Artillery and Combat veteran who had not been FDR's choice to be Vice President. Good fortune and an act of providence bestowed the huge burden upon a studious and highly regarded gentleman. Though Truman never took the bar exam, he had attended law school, giving him the knowledge necessary to read legislation presented to him to sign into law. No one was going to run a whizzer on Harry, and if they did, he was man enough to accept it as his mistake. A sign on his desk read "The Buck Stops Here."

Truman, who had been a successful farmer and haberdasher for several years in his early life, was possessed of more than a little common sense and a somewhat testy personality. Roosevelt had never confided in Truman, never briefed him on the military matters of World War II, nor about the Manhattan Project and the Atom Bomb. Truman took sole responsibility when he ordered the first bomb to be dropped. His first concern was saving the lives of Allied servicemen and women who would have been forced to invade the mainland of Japan. Both a noble and courageous act.

There are those detractors who blame Truman for forging our ties with Israel. Truman was the first to send a congratulatory message within a quarter hour after David Ben Gurion declared the formation of the state of Israel on May 14, 1948.[30]

Truman's domestic policies at first followed closely those of FDR, but later, Truman became his own man and his policies became known as The Fair Deal. His presidency was witness to some spectacular successes. The Truman Doctrine, preventing the Soviet takeover of Greece, the Marshall Plan brought about a spectacular economic recovery of Europe, and the 1948 Berlin Airlift broke the back of the Soviet blockade of Berlin. The creation of NATO was another bright spot for Harry Truman.[33]

The presidential election of 1948 was surely the brightest star in Truman's crown. He defeated a flamboyant and cocky Thomas Dewey. Most if not all the major newspapers ran a premature headline announcing "Dewey Wins." Whoa, hold your horses! Harry Truman had pulled off an unprecedented and spectacular upset. Some of Truman's brightest moments lay ahead.

When the communist North Koreans attacked South Korea in June 1950, Truman, with the concurrence of all his military advisors, made "Korea Harry Truman's war. Under a severe time constraint, the President acted without seeking the consent of Congress or the American people. Truman admonished Dean Acheson, his secretary of state, with these words: "Dean, we've got to stop the sons of bitches, no matter what, and that's all there is to it."[34]

The Korean conflict brought General Douglas MacArthur back into military command. As cocky as ever and as brilliant, MacArthur's 'impossible' attack on Inchon turned the tide. Though United Nations forces fought valiantly into North Korea and up to the Yalu River, a massive attack by Chinese communist forces across the frozen Yalu prompted the UN troops to retreat all the way back to South Korea.

General MacArthur had, in violation of orders to the contrary, lobbied Congress for authority to attack across the Yalu in an effort to neutralize the many Chinese airbases that based many hundreds—if not thousands—of the superior MiG-15 jet fighters. These supersonic aircraft crossed into North Korea to attack UN fighters, support Chinese and North Korean ground forces, and return back across the Chinese boundary without fear of being followed.

MacArthur's un-military conduct drew the ire of Truman. The president summoned the general to meet on Wake Island, a midway point chosen by Truman so that MacArthur could get back to the war zone quickly. MacArthur arrived late became more and more irritating to the president.

Finally, fed up with MacArthur's posturing and disregard of orders, and noting the concerns of our UN Allies, Truman insisted on April 6, 1951, "I'm going to fire the son of a bitch right now". MacArthur was ordered to turnover his command at once to Lieutenant General Matthew B. Ridgway. General Bradley warned Truman that if MacArthur heard about the orders before they reached him officially, he might resign with an arrogant flair. Truman exclaimed, "The son of a bitch isn't going to resign on me, I want him fired." MacArthur's dismissal was announced on late night radio.[34]

The Korean War dragged on until 1953 when an armistice—never a peace treaty—was signed. Truman, to his eternal credit, insured that the conflict did not become World War III.

General Dwight David Eisenhower became the thirty-fourth president, following a brilliant military career, his last and most prestigious command being that as Commander-in-Chief, Allied Forces Europe and overall planner of the D-Day Invasion and final occupation of Germany. Eisenhower's foreign relations policy was to prevent an accidental or even intentional missile strike either by our forces or those of the Soviet Union.

Eisenhower's domestic policies virtually followed those of FDR and Truman. His real love and avocation was a gentlemanly round of golf anywhere. His administration was not spectacular, but America stayed safe and secure. We can thank the Eisenhower for the Interstate System.

On January 20, 1961, John Fitzgerald Kennedy was inaugurated as our youngest president and first Roman Catholic. JFK was a questionable hero of World War II, a charismatic figure, and the first knight of the new Camelot. He had a gorgeous wife and two beautiful, energetic children. JFK also had a wandering eye and a penchant for the lovely ladies who were drawn readily to him, his charm, and his good looks. "He was nearly a pathological philanderer and was usually incapable of viewing a woman as anything but a sex object." O'Brien, Michael (2011-12-16). John F. Kennedy's Women: The Story of a Sexual Obsession (Kindle Locations 17-18). Now and Then Reader, LLC. Kindle Edition.

Though he had his human frailties, he was actually a more-than-competent administrator. He appointed his brother Bobby as his attorney general. They were a far better team than our current duo. The Kennedy family draws tragedy unerringly to its core. JFK was no exception; he was assassinated in Dallas, Texas on November 22, 1963.

JFK's successor, Lyndon Baines Johnson, was immediately sworn into office to thwart any planned coup. Johnson was an arrogant, bossy, know-it-all who had served far too long in Congress before being picked as JFK's running mate. LBJ's social agenda was known as the Great Society. Johnson worked his way through the ranks, was elected to the House where he served six terms, and was elected to the Senate in

1948, the year Truman beat Dewey. In 1953, Johnson became the youngest minority leader in Senate history. His political acumen and arm-twisting skills helped President Eisenhower obtain the passage of many key measures.

"In 1964, Johnson won the Presidency with 61 percent of the vote and had the widest popular margin in American history—more than 15,000,000 votes." [35]

Johnson attempted to pass the measures Kennedy had wanted—a new civil rights bill and a tax cut. He then urged the nation to "build a great society, a place where the meaning of man's life matches the marvels of man's labor." Those words are so unlike the really unpleasant and apparently jealous successor to a chivalrous Kennedy. Johnson too had a penchant for the easy ladies. He reportedly kept females on staff in the White House to provide him sexual favors whenever he desired. Not a nice man and not a laudable head of state and government.

Johnson was responsible for the Medicare Amendment to the Social Security Act. Johnson was a staunch supporter of the space program from its very inception. His administration was troubled by racial tensions in spite of the fact that new anti-discrimination and anti-poverty programs had been enacted. Race riots in big city ghettos were troublesome. Johnson was anti-segregation and for law and order but there was to be no early or easy solution.

The war in Vietnam had begun in 1953 and when France via NATO asked America to defend French interests in Southeast Asia, Eisenhower acceded to their request because "Eisenhower did not want communism to spread throughout the world and eventually to America." Johnson startled the world when he announced that he would not be a candidate for reelection; he was intent on pursuing peace in Vietnam. On its face, that was a magnanimous gesture. However, Johnson and his secretary of defense, Robert McNamara, were not prepared, either by military training or by experience to micromanage the conflict as they attempted to do. The conflict was ultimately resolved by the North Vietnamese overrunning South Vietnam. Arrogance is a proper adjective for Lyndon Baines Johnson.[36]

The Vietnam War—the most unpopular war in which America has become involved—resulted in a huge civilian backlash, the loss of life for protestors, and a mass draft-dodging exodus to Canada. The American troops—who had fought so courageously under terrible conditions and the relegation of senior commanders—came home to terrible personal treatment by the angry, insufferable anti-war protestors.

Johnson did not live to see the end of the conflict. He suffered a fatal heart attack at his ranch in Texas on January 22, 1973.

Meanwhile, Richard Milhouse Nixon, after a previous run and a narrow defeat by JFK in 1960, finally won the presidential election in 1968 with Spiro Agnew as his Vice President. Nixon's domestic agenda resulted in the end to the draft, revenue sharing, new anti-crime laws, and a broad environmental program. He and Henry Kissinger were able to reach a peace accord with North Vietnam that ended America's involvement in Indochina.

America made its first moon landing during Nixon's first term. Not a bad start for a man not easily understood. He lacked the touch of the common man, more the monarchial type.

Nixon was reelected by a huge margin over his Democratic rival, George McGovern. Shortly thereafter, the bottom fell out. Watergate became the crime of the century, at least to the left wing media. Unrelated scandals in Maryland forced Agnew to resign; he was replaced by Gerald Ford. Ford became president when, under threat of impeachment, Nixon resigned on August 9, 1974.

Ford became president and immediately drew the ire of the media, the Democrats, and a huge portion of the American citizenry when he pardoned Nixon for his crimes. Gerald Ford was regarded as a genuinely nice man with a penchant for tripping over his own feet. Though a star football player in his collegiate days, he was the worst golfer to show up on the local Washington courses. Ford's domestic and foreign programs bore out his self-description, "a moderate in domestic affairs, a conservative in fiscal affairs, and a dyed-in-the-wool internationalist in foreign affairs" (http://www.whitehouse.gov/about/presidents/Gerald ford).

Jimmy Carter graduated from the United States Naval Academy in 1946 with a generic bachelor of science degree, fifty-ninth in a class of 820. He served with little distinction for seven years and then went home to Georgia to enter politics. He became governor in 1970. He was strong on ecology and efficiency in government, and set about removing racial barriers. His efforts drew the attention of the new young Southern governors and Carter announced his plans to run for the presidency in 1974.

At the 1974 Democratic National Convention, he was nominated on the first ballot, chose Walter Mondale as his vice-presidential running mate, and in the general election, defeated Gerald Ford 297 to 241 electoral votes. At his inaugural, Carter praised Ford thusly, "For myself and for our nation, I want to thank my predecessor for all he has done to heal our land." A grateful nation agreed.

Carter's stated ambition was to make government "competent and compassionate." Competency was not his forte. Contrary to his claims of streamlining and downsizing the state government of Georgia while he was governor, there were claims that his efficiencies were all talk, nothing more. Carter managed to establish a national energy policy and created the Department of Education that has had no enduring success. To his credit, he appointed record numbers of women, blacks, and Hispanics to government jobs.[37]

To his everlasting discredit, one of his first acts was to grant amnesty to the American draft dodgers who fled to Canada to avoid having to serve in Vietnam. It is a festering thorn in the side of those men and women who did serve in Indochina. Carter's major calamity was the understudied, undermanned, and belated attempt to rescue fifty-two American hostages held by the Iranian government for 444 days…

Carter's popularity as a president and his efficiency rating are absolute bottom tier. Only history will tell whether Carter or Obama takes the title "worst ever."

Ronald Wilson Reagan was born in 1911 in Tampico, Illinois. After graduating from Dixon High in Tampico, Ronald Reagan matriculated at Eureka College. He worked his way through college, majoring in economics and sociology. He played football and had a lifelong interest in sports. When he graduated from Eureka, he became a radio sports announcer. His good looks, personality, and speaking voice landed him a screen test; following which, he appeared in over fifty movies.

Reagan was active in the politics of the movie industry, ultimately becoming president of the Screen Actors Guild. In that capacity, he became involved in disputes over communism in the industry. Up until this point, Reagan had been a Democrat with very liberal views. The disputes over communism in the film industry caused him to change his viewpoint and become much more conservative. Ronald Reagan was an extremely outgoing and popular individual; so much so that he was ultimately convinced to run for the governorship of the state of California. He won his first race in 1966, convincingly by over one million votes. He was reelected in 1970, still popular and charismatic.

Reagan easily won the 1980 Republican nomination for president, chose former Texas Congressman and UN ambassador George H. W. Bush as his running mate. The team won a convincing victory; 489 electoral votes to Carter's 49. The American hostages who had been held by the Iranian government were released on January 20, 1981, President Ronald Reagan's inaugural day. Mr. Reagan was off to a fantastic start.

However, just sixty-nine days later, President Reagan was shot by a would-be assassin. The assassin, John Hinckley was just another wanna-be with a juvenile crush on a movie actress, trying to make a name for himself. Fortunately, President Reagan survived and set about doing his business getting America back on her feet. Jimmy Carter's economic policies had wreaked havoc with our economy. The Reaganomics policies of Mr. Reagan ultimately straightened out the American economy.

By the end of his administration, the nation was enjoying its longest recorded period of peace and prosperity without recession or depression. His administration was not without problems; the Iran-Contra scandal could have been disastrous, but nobody other than the Democrats had any desire to besmirch the name and reputation of Ronald Wilson Reagan.

President Reagan's vice president, George H. W. Bush was a World War II hero of sorts, having been shot down in his torpedo bomber in the Pacific, for which he was awarded the distinguished Flying Cross. Before becoming president, George Bush had served in numerous important governmental capacities and had traveled extensively in foreign countries. He was well-known and well-respected by foreign leaders. President Bush's tenure was beset by numerous problems, among them President Manuel Noriega of Panama was threatening the Panama Canal and Americans living there. President Bush sent troops into Panama to capture Noriega. He was brought back to the United States, tried, and ultimately, imprisoned.

In the Middle East, greater problems arose. Dictator Saddam Hussein of Iraq invaded his neighbor, Kuwait. President Bush asked Congress for support, which he received. In an operation known as Desert Storm, American forces under the control of General Norman Schwarzkopf annihilated the forces of Hussein in a hundred days. President Bush decided not to push his advantage and go after Hussein, who became a permanent thorn in the Middle East.

All in all, President Bush was a popular and capable president. However, he made one fatal error on television. During the 1988 presidential convention, Mr. Bush assured the American people by saying, "Read my lips, no new taxes." Of course, given the economy, he was forced to raise taxes that ultimately, as one would expect, did not go over too well with the American people. Rather than becoming a two-term president and continuing the policies set down by President Reagan, Mr. Bush was defeated by William Jefferson Clinton. I went for a spoiler vote: Ross Perot.

I could never have voted for Clinton. His reputation as attorney general and governor of Arkansas were textbook lessons in crooked government, drugs, and debauchery. William "Bill" Clinton was the quintessential slick politician. He was handsome, well-educated, and a Rhoades scholar. Too bad he had that unscrupulous hippie mentality. He always hung around with the musicians—understandable since he was an accomplished saxophone player.

His spouse, Hillary, was of the hippie persuasion also; and had a reputation for being foul-mouthed and bossy. Hillary had a reputation for swearing at her security personnel while she was First Lady in Little Rock. Both she and Bill were lawyers, both very bright, and both ostensibly untrustworthy. However, during Clinton's first term, the country enjoyed more peace and economic well-being than at any time in our history; according to his recently revised White House biography,

NOTE: "The Presidential biographies on www. whitehouse.gov are from "The Presidents of the United States of America," by Michael Beschless and Hugh Sidey. Copyright 2009 by the White House Historical Association." These presidential biographies were reworked by Obama's crew to reflect most favorably on Democrats and to denigrate Republicans.

Clinton was the first Democrat since FDR to be elected for a second term. He could claim the lowest unemployment rate in modern times, the lowest inflation rate in thirty years, and the highest home ownership in the country's history. He proposed the first balanced budget in decades and achieved a budget surplus. The United States Military was skeletonized in order to balance the budget.

Congress turned back Clinton's vaunted, Hillary-guided, health care program. This despite the fact that for the first time in twelve years, the Democrats held both Houses of Congress.

That changed when, in the 1994 midterm elections, the Republicans won both houses. Newt Gingrich, as Speaker of the House presented the Contract with America, written by Larry Hunter and Gingrich. It resonated well with Americans.

The lecherous Clinton—so intelligent and so capable—had an ongoing sexual liaison with a White House intern. The House impeached Clinton, only the second president to be so humiliated. He apologized to the nation, but there is a lingering suspicion that there was much more to his conduct than was presented to the nation.

Nevertheless, Clinton remained—and remains—relatively popular, and his advice is sought by all the active Democratic politicians in Washington.

The election of 2000 between George W. Bush (the son of G. H.W. Bush) and Al Gore, Clinton's Vice President went all the way to the Supreme Court before the final vote in Florida was awarded to Bush. He then became our forty-third president and only the second whose father had held that high office. The Democrats, as is their usual behavior, claimed they were robbed of the Florida electoral votes. Gore did win the popular vote though by 543, 895 votes. I voted for Bush, both in 2000 and in 2004.

Bush was sworn in on January 20, 2001. The left-wing media began their battle to discredit the Bush victory in Florida and any loss they blame on a Republican they could remotely denigrate. The Bush national and foreign policy programs had just begun when, on September 11, 2001, Muslim terrorists flew hijacked commercial airliners into the World Trade Center, into the Pentagon and—had it not been for the courage of passengers on United Airlines flight 93 who overpowered the hijackers—it may have crashed possibly into the Capitol Building.[38]

Following the attacks, George Sr. remarked his son had faced the greatest challenge of any president since Abraham Lincoln.

In response to the 9/11 attacks, President Bush formed the new cabinet-level Department of Homeland Security and sent troops into Afghanistan to break up the Taliban under the leadership of Osama bin Laden. Bin Laden was elusive and was still running free when Dubya's first term ended. During this period, Bush also realigned our intelligence gathering and analysis agencies. He also delivered on his campaign promises to cut taxes.

The most controversial act during his first term was, with the approval of Congress, to send troops into Iraq, believing that Saddam Hussein was in possession of weapons of mass destruction (WMD) and thereby posed a grave threat to the United States. In a massive operation known as Iraqi Freedom, Saddam Hussein was driven into hiding, ultimately captured, tried by the Iraqis, and hanged.

No WMDs were ever found. However, a Soviet MiG-21 was found buried in sand in the vast Iraqi desert. Could caches of WMD also be buried in that vast area?

Bush was challenged in the 2004 presidential election by Senator John Kerry, a veteran of Vietnam and the recipient of suspect awards for valor and for wounds received. Bush won that contest 51 percent to 48 for Kerry.

Bush was not popular with the mainstream media. They went so far as to attempt to discredit his Air National Guard time as a draft dodging scheme. or simply a means of avoiding service in Vietnam. One major network anchor, Dan Rather, claimed to have records proving that Bush did not fulfill his service commitments. Rather was never able to produce more than a Xerox copy, when originals are a must. Rather was forced to retire. We shall see more regarding this when I analyze, summarize, and connect a few dots further down the line.

The fiasco called the presidential campaign of 2008 introduced a virtual unknown into the Democratic primary race. He was a long, lanky, half-white from Illinois serving his first term as a United States senator. He came on like gangbusters. Barack Hussein Obama was brash, articulate, and annoying with an arrogant, narcissistic, nose-high attitude. So who in hell is he? We shall see.

The Democratic primary contest began with Senator Joe Biden, Senator Hillary Clinton, Senator Christopher Dodd, former Senator John Williams, former Senator Mike Gravel, Representative Dennis Kucinich, and Governor Bill Richardson. There were others who had considered, talked about, and disappeared before making the run. Most dropped out following the Iowa caucuses and, on June 3, Obama became the presumptive Democratic nominee when he had received 2118 delegates, according to reporting news sources. Obama had quite handily beaten the conventional Democratic candidates.

Obama selected Joe Biden as his vice-presidential running mate to face the Republican candidate, Arizona senator John McCain and his VP choice, Sarah Palin. So, who is Barack Obama? He is remarkably and unexpectedly our forty-fourth president-to-be come January 20, 2009. No, I did not vote for this wiseacre. I really voted for Sarah Palin. John McCain had become that dreaded persona, a Republican in Name Only (RINO).

On January 20, 2009, Barack Hussein Obama was duly sworn into office and immediately began making enemies. His White House Presidential entry is questionable; it is so egotistically presented.[39] He is assuredly the master of the Teleprompter; unable to speak clearly without it.

THE FORCES AT WORK

As noted earlier, our first six presidents were basically honorable and trustworthy men. Most were large landowners, bankers, and businessmen and comprised a political entity known as the Federalists. They never registered as a political party, and thus, not a faction. There were associated individuals known as the Anti-Federalists, active in friendly opposition to the Federalists. They too never registered themselves as a political party and by 1792 were no longer a political entity.

Thomas Jefferson likely sowed the first seeds of discord when his Democratic-Republican Party went national. Jefferson and Madison started the Democratic-Republican Party as a caucus in the House of Representatives and then spread to every state to contest elections and to oppose the programs of secretary for the treasury, Alexander Hamilton.

Alexander Hamilton was a well-educated young man, born out of wedlock in the West Indies in 1757. He was sent to New York for schooling and became one of New York's most influential attorneys. He wrote fifty-one of the eighty-five Federalist papers and played a leading role in the Constitutional Convention. The United States, utilizing Hamilton's novel financial system was soon the best credit risk in the entire western world.

The United States faced a huge national debt when Hamilton proposed the government assume the nation's debt and that of the several states. Hamilton planned to retire depreciated obligations and borrow money at lower rates. Debt-free states objected and for six months, a bitter debate raged in Congress. Jefferson and Madison brought about a compromise in which Hamilton agreed to build the new nation's capital on the banks of the Potomac River in the south, between Maryland and Virginia.

Hamilton's debt program was a huge success. European money flowed into the new nation in vast amounts. [40]

So where was the problem? A national bank was the problem. Hamilton proposed such a bank to collect taxes, safeguard the nation's funds, and make loans to the government and borrowers. A viable criticism was that such a bank was *un-Republican*. It would encourage speculation and corruption.

Jefferson and Madison argued that such a bank was unconstitutional since the Constitution did not *specifically* give Congress the power to create a bank. Further, Hamilton proposed high tariffs to protect American industry from foreign competition. This notion was in direct conflict with Jefferson's vision of an agrarian America, with a nation of farmers communing with nature and maintaining personal freedom through land ownership.

Hamilton's vision differed in that it had no place for slavery, a prosperous enterprise necessary to the agricultural economy of the South in the production of tobacco, cotton, rice, and indigo.

Jefferson's down-home appeal drew the rural agrarian voter to his Democratic-Republican Party. The framers of the constitution never had in mind a system of government with political parties. Even Jefferson once remarked, "If I could not go to heaven but with a party, I would not go there at all."[41]

Party politics is the first mistake that the fledgling United States permitted to infect the political body. Our Founding Fathers had hoped that the better sort of citizens would debate the key issues and reach a harmonious conclusion how best to govern the nation.

On that basis, the founders developed a form of government not wholly democratic, thus heeding the warnings of so many philosophers beginning with Plato in *the Republic*. "Plato's thoughts on democracy were that it causes the corruption of people through public opinion and creates rulers who do not actually know how to rule but only know how to influence the "beast" which is the Demos, the public. The Greek Philosopher Plato suggested n his "Republic" the people, the 'Demos' are corrupted by incompetent rulers. One of the framers was Benjamin Franklin, at the conclusion of the 1787 Constitutional Convention, a lady asked Dr. Franklin, "Well, Doctor, what have we got, a republic or a monarchy?" "A republic," replied the doctor, "if you can keep it."[44]

Ben Franklin was a very wise, well-read, and well-traveled man. In the intervening 225 years since Dr. Franklin's documented warning, unscrupulous, greedy, incompetent, and power-hungry politicians have succeeded in forcing this great dream to the brink of destruction. The very first, but unforeseen, crack in the foundation was the formation of the Democratic-Republican Party by Thomas Jefferson and James Madison around 1791. It was formed specifically to oppose the fiscal policies of Hamilton. The first signs of perpetual friction were now in place.

Jefferson was the first president with a defined political party affiliation when he was elected in 1800. Jefferson had served first as Washington's secretary of state. His sympathy for the French Revolution conflicted with treasury secretary Hamilton's beliefs; and Jefferson resigned.

Jefferson came within three votes of being elected in 1796 and, through a flaw in the Constitution, became John Adam's vice president, though Jefferson was an opponent of Adams. The Congress was forced to break the impasse. The Republican electors wanted the president and vice president to be members of the same constituency. The vote was a tie, broken by Hamilton in favor of Jefferson. Of course, Hamilton was no friend of Aaron Burr, Jefferson's opponent. History records that Burr evened the score against Hamilton with a duel on the Weehawken Heights in New Jersey in which he killed Hamilton.

To keep the office of the chief executive in perspective, George Washington, Thomas Jefferson, James Madison, and James Monroe each served eight years, while both John Adams and his son John Quincy served only four years.

Now the trouble begins. Andrew "Old Hickory" Jackson, with the aid of powerful allies, won the White House in 1828. Party and dirty power politics became an everlasting reality for the once genteel and courteous American people. State political machines were being built on patronage. "To the victor belongs the spoils" is the famous quote by New York Senator William Learned Marcy (1786–1857), recited in the US Senate on January 25, 1832. The spoils system became popularly used.[45]

To his credit, "Jackson took a milder view. Decrying officeholders who seemed to enjoy life tenure, he believed Government duties could be "so plain and simple" that offices should rotate among deserving applicants." This would appear to be a vote for term limits as far back as 1830.[46]

Jackson was the first president *not* to defer to Congress in making policy. He made use of the veto and his party leadership to take command. He was often referred to as King Andrew I, not without cause. Jackson hated the Second National Bank and vowed to "kill it," which he did. He later vetoed legislation that would have established a third bank with a charter for twenty years, similar to banks one and two.

Party politics is not only a nasty, degrading, and disgraceful method of shifting power; it has lead to disgraceful, unlawful, and heinous actions, including gross misconduct, bribery, grand theft, misuse of government property, conspiracy, use of federal employees to further unlawful policies, lying on a grand scale, suspicion of murder, and even murder.[47] [48] [49]

How were citizens made aware of the day-to-day happenings in the political arena? One might reason that newspapers reported the news on a daily basis. That would be only partially correct. The first attempt at a newspaper was printed on three of four sheets of 6 × 10 pages of a folded sheet of paper. It was printed by Richard Pierce and edited by Benjamin Harris in Boston on September 25, 1690.

There was only one issue printed, and it was done without government permission. Therefore, it was suppressed, the publisher arrested, and all but one copy destroyed. A surviving copy was later found in the British Library. The Bill of Rights would have prevented that. This story and a short history of newspapers in America may be found at the following link:[50]

The first attempt at serious journalism in America appeared in the *New England Courant* first issued on August 7, 1721. The paper was founded by James Franklin, the older brother of Ben Franklin. It was published in Boston, a major city in Colonial America. Franklin's friends advised him not to publish the paper. However, James was a courageous man and was dissatisfied with others' earlier attempts—which lacked proper syntax and correct grammar—to publish a quality paper.

The language of Franklin's *Courant* set the tenor for the next one hundred years or so in American journalism. The courant consisted of a single sheet of paper and was printed on both sides. It contained shipping reports, news from neighboring towns, and letters from Europe. "Its real substance was in letters to the editor from the Boston wits, poking fun at the city's morals and manners."[51]

After 1750, general news became readily available, and newspapers began to show more and more interest in public affairs. The *Massachusetts Spy*, published in Worchester by Isaiah Thomas, was constantly on the verge of being suppressed. It carried articles from other papers and was considered quite radical.

It laid the groundwork for one of the great works published (anonymously at first) in America, such as *Common Sense* by Thomas Paine in 1776. Paine spoke the language of the common man. His work struck sympathetic chords and became a battle cry for revolution. The power of the press can hardly be denied, whether the words are good or bad. Paine wrote in the introduction, paragraph 4, line 1: "cause of America is in a great measure the cause of all mankind." Paine, Thomas (2009-06-20). Common Sense ($.99 Patriot Classics–Complete Original Text) (Kindle Locations 11-12). Kindle Edition.

The time between 1775 and 1783 was turbulent. It proved to be a real trial for the few newspapers being published. There were thirty-seven when the battle of Lexington occurred, forty-three when the treaty was signed, but only a dozen remained in operation between those two events. Not one paper in Boston, New York, or Philadelphia continued to publish throughout the war.

Equipment for publishing a newspaper was in short supply, worn-out type could not be replaced, paper became scarce, and the most able and skilled writers were occupied elsewhere. The Declaration of Independence was published by Congress on July 6, 1776, in the *Philadelphia Evening Post* from which it was copied by other papers. Full accounts of the war were scarce, seldom found in the contemporaneous newspapers. Newspapers did, however, report quite faithfully the proceedings of governmental bodies.

"The general spirit of the time found fuller utterance in mottoes, editorials, letters, and poems. In the beginning both editorials and communications urged united resistance to oppression, praised patriotism, and denounced tyranny; as events and public sentiment developed these grew more vigorous, often a little more radical than the populace."[52]

When Alexander Hamilton, James Madison, and John Jay began writing the Federalist papers, they chose to publish them in the *Independent Journal* and the *Daily Advertiser.* They were then copied by nearly every paper in America before being finally printed in book form. The print media—book, pamphlet or newspaper—became the lifeblood of politics long before the advent of electronic media.

When Congress first assembled on March 4, 1789, the administration felt the need of a federal newspaper to report the conduct of official government business. Alexander Hamilton acquired the services of one John Fenno of New York, who issued the first *Gazette of the United States*—the earliest of a set of administrative organs—on April 15, 1789.

The First Party System was taking shape during the last decade of the eighteenth century. Partisan bitterness came to the fore and newspapers were all too happy to oblige. New England papers were predominantly Federalist, Pennsylvania somewhat more neutral, and the Republican press dominated in the south and the west.

The *Gazette of the United States* followed the government move to Philadelphia in 1790 and became the eye of the storm when Thomas Jefferson accused the *Gazette* of being, "a paper of pure Toryism, disseminating the doctrines of monarchy, aristocracy, and the exclusion of the people." Ibid.

The party system of politics and the partisanship of political news reporting begun so early in our history still persist to this day. The same vitriol, gross exaggeration, and outright prevarication are the norm. Add the television news organizations to the mix and you get questionable accuracy in news reports, acerbic A.D. hominem attacks by "celebrity" hacks, opinions rather than facts, and provable outright lies.

AN ANALOGY TO GAIN
PERSPECTIVE

When illness strikes, the remedy may be mildly, moderately, or extremely painful. There may be lingering discomfort from the treatment or from the underlying illness or condition. Either situation is necessary for recovery to a state of optimal health.

During World War II, this writer served in the China-Burma-India theater of operations. My unit was based in Calcutta, West Bengal, India. My function was that of an army tugboat captain. We would travel into the Bay of Bengal, through the Sundarban Delta, and north along the numerous rivers of what is now Bangladesh. The entire area is wet tropical, humid, and hot. It was my misfortune to contract some ailments endemic to the area: dengue or break-bone fever, three separate instances, amoebic dysentery, and armpit boils.

For my analogy, amoebic dysentery is choice number one. First, it is or can be life-threatening. It sometimes is difficult to detect in early stages, and the treatment is quite painful with the recovery period fairly long. Once diagnosed, I was hospitalized immediately, put into a hospital bed for the duration of the initial phase of treatment.

The only treatment at that time was a regimen of injections of emetine, once in the morning of the first day, scheduled for one injection in the buttocks each day for six successive days, *unless* the medication caused likely serious side effects. Of course, mine did. Unknown to me, following the fourth injection, tests indicated the medication was causing a deleterious effect on my cardiovascular system. Shot number five was a half dose as was number six.

Each injection caused the injection site to swell to the size and shape of half a grapefruit. It was extremely painful, and it remained painful for the duration of the treatment and for about a week afterward. My treatment was now eight shots; succeeding injections were directly into one of the half-grapefruit-sized swellings.

After eight days, I was told to report to a therapist outside my ward for the start of my recuperation, which was expected to take about two weeks. Volleyball was the first exercise recommended. Shortly after beginning, I jumped up and a little to the rear, fell on my swollen buttocks and painfully bounced right back to my feet. I was more careful from then on. Volleyball and jogging were the bulk of the therapy. It worked; the swelling and the pain disappeared.

I was pronounced dysentery-free and returned to base with a note for my commanding officer. The CO informed me that the doctor's note recommended that I be sent up to the Darjeeling Rest Camp for two weeks to gain back some strength. Darjeeling was the center of the tea-growing region in the Himalayas and was at an elevation of some eight thousand feet.

I packed some uniforms and was trucked to the Howrah Station on the west side of the Hooghly River. I met a few GIs from other units also headed for Darjeeling. It was about a six-hour ride on the narrow gauge railway up to Darjeeling. We arrived in late afternoon, checked in, had chow, took a short sightseeing stroll around town, and learned quickly that—coming from sea level to over eight thousand feet—simply walking around was a real test of endurance.

I sacked out early and awoke a few hours later, suffering sharp to dull pain in both armpits. I went into the latrine, looked at both armpits, and saw that both were badly swollen. We had been instructed not to go out anywhere alone after dark, so I awakened one of the GIs I had been with on the train to walk with me to the dispensary. My armpits were extremely painful, so I placed my hands on top of my head to ease the pain.

At the dispensary, the medic on duty, a staff sergeant, took one look and said, "Damn, Sergeant, you have seven boils under one arm and eight under the other."

I asked, "How do you treat them?"

He replied, "Sarge, you aren't going to like this, but it has to be done. I have to lance each one individually and squeeze all the pus out."

I said, "Let's do it."

He put several lancets and a pile of gauze on a stainless steel tray, then told me to put both hands on top of my head, grit my teeth, and try not to move.

I did as he directed. He picked up a lancet, dipped the point in what I assumed to be alcohol, turned, and asked, "Ready?

I nodded and he stuck that lancet about an inch deep into the head of one of the boils. I know I let out a hard grunt at the pain. A large amount of pus shot out of the wound and the medic placed some gauze over the boil and squeezed. Tears came to my eyes, but I can honestly say, I never moved or cried out.

The medic asked, "You okay?"

I replied, "Yep!"

That same procedure took place fourteen more times within about an hour. Finally, the sergeant took a dozen or so gauze pads, applied what he called a drawing ointment, and taped the whole thing into one armpit. He repeated the procedure on the other side and sent me back to my billets with instructions to return early the next morning. He gave me a couple of pills for the pain and my friend and I went back to our billets.

I slept well and when I awoke, the pain was gone. Before going to breakfast, I went to the dispensary. The same medic was there and he asked, "How did it go last night?"

I told him everything went okay. He told me to take off my jacket so he could examine his handiwork. He removed the gauze packs, both full of residue on top of the ointment. He wiped both armpits with large gauze wipes and said, "Well, I'll be damned, no sign of any more infection."

He said, "Go take a shower, pay particular attention to the armpits, and then come back and let me check them later this evening."

I did as he instructed and surprisingly, there was little to no pain as I washed the areas.

When I checked back at the dispensary, the sergeant took a good look and told me I was good to go. To this day, I have never had another boil. The cure was to brutal and messy to say the least, but it worked. The time from diagnosis through treatment took less than one full day. That is pretty efficient and enduring.

Both ailments and their treatments are analogous to our national problems and the remedies needed. Let's take a look back at where most of the damage began. Andrew Jackson had a notion that he had been a popularly elected president. He had a desire for revenge against the J. Q. Adams bureaucracy, claiming it was fraudulent and angry because Adams's people had—according to Jackson—worked against him in the election.

Jackson was responsible for the Indian massacres in Alabama and for the Trail of Tears removal of Eastern Indian tribes to reservations in the west. Jackson fired many high-ranking Washington officials claiming he was "purging the corruption, laxity, and arrogance that came with long tenure, and restoring the opportunity for government service to the citizenry at large through 'rotation in office.'"[52]

Jackson righteously claimed he was reforming a corrupt government; however, his reforms smacked more of revenge than of reform. Jackson had a favorable Congress and was not afraid to use some muscle to accomplish his goals. Jackson made frequent use of his veto power.

Jackson doled out offices as rewards, the most notorious being that of Samuel Swartwout, an old army buddy and political sycophant whom Jackson appointed—against all recommendations—to be the collector of the New York City customhouse where the government collected nearly half its annual revenue. Swartwout absconded with more than $1 million. In 1838, that was a huge sum. Jackson never sought his apprehension and courtroom justice.

http://www.cbp.gov/xp/cgov/about/history/did_you_know/samuel_swartwout/sam_swartwout.xml

Obviously, the Twenty-Fifth Congress was lax in its oversight. Jackson was an arrogant, dictatorial idiot who should have been trumped by congressional action. Jackson's spoils system was endemic to his administration and could have been cured by a quick injection of contempt proceedings or impeachment.

Jackson's governance initiated the epidemic of maladministration that led to the virtually untenable political and economic situation we face today. Early intervention would have served as a warning to the next few generations of politicians who became crooked administrators.

Had the Sixty-Third Congress—which was seated on April 7, 1913—been more vigilant, Woodrow Wilson may have been unable to carry out his horrendous, unlawful, and unjustifiable deeds. They ultimately led us into an ill-fated and disastrous European war and into an untenable banking liaison which ultimately led to the Federal Reserve Bank, a millstone around the neck of our economy.

The First Session of the Seventy-Third Congress met before the official seating occurred. It met on Franklin Roosevelt's order on what would be later known as the Hundred Days for the specific purpose of passing two pieces of legislation. The first was the

Emergency Banking Act, which provided for the Treasury Department to initiate reserve requirements and a federal bailout to large failing institutions. The EBA also removed the United States from the Gold Standard.

The second was the Economy Act of 1933 which, if not passed, according to FDR, would force the country to face a billion-dollar deficit. The Economy Act balanced the federal budget by cutting the salaries of government employees and cutting pensions to veterans by as much as 15 percent.

http://en.wikipedia.org/wiki/73rd_United_States_Congress#Major_events

Bad governance by particular administrations has been covered previously. Let us now examine the bad acts by the current forty-fourth president of the United States. I must confess, it galls me to speak of Barack Hussein Obama as our president. It galls me more that, in my view, the 111th and 112th Congresses have acquiesced to an individual who may well be the greatest imposter of all time.

He was poorly vetted by the Democratic Party, was and is possessed of virtually no presidential credentials (other than adherence to the credo of the liberal traditionalists), caters to a sycophantic news media and fringe elements, thereby fostering notions not in consonance with mainstream Christian America.

Mr. Obama and the 111th Congress forced onto the American public a law, the Patient Protection and Affordable Care Act (PPACA) generally and disgustedly referred to as Obamacare. This law and the Health Care and Education Reconciliation Act of 2010 are the principal healthcare reform legislation and nearly the entire output of the 111th Congress. It is and was such an abominable piece of legislation that even the arrogant Democratic Speaker of the House Nancy Pelosi, smirking obscenely, remarked, "We have to get it passed so we can see what's in it." That remark was in one sense very appropriate because at over three thousand pages in so short a time, and with so many amendments and do-overs, no one could have read or understood the entire content.

http://www.newsrealblog.com/2010/12/27/top-10-most-outrageous-quotes-from-nancy-pelosi/

Warnings that Obamacare is unconstitutional did not deter Obama or the Democrats, who backed Obama in his effort to force an undesirable piece of legislation onto an angry American public.

This argument will ultimately be decided by an impartial Supreme Court. I believe they will be impartial, with the exception of Justice Elena Kagan, who—most legal minds believe—should have recused herself. Why? Here's why. "federal law, 28 USC 455, says a Supreme Court justice must recuse from "any proceeding in which his impartiality might reasonably be questioned" or anytime he has "expressed an opinion concerning the merits of the particular case in controversy" while he "served in governmental employment."

http://cnsnews.com/news/article/kagan-sits-judgment-obamacare-despite-cheering-its-passage-and-assigning-lawyer-defend

Mr. Obama has multiple problems with the United States Constitution, none of which can or will be resolved until several different cases are heard by that court.

Just to point out a few, let's look as Arizona's SB 1070, their attempt to resolve their illegal immigration problems. Almost immediately following Governor Brewer's signing SB 1070 into law, Obama and his attorney general, Eric Holder—both self-proclaimed constitutional scholars—informed her that only the federal government could pass laws regarding immigration.

Justice Joseph Story wrote the definitive study and explanation of the United States Constitution in 1865, entitled, A Familiar Exposition of the Constitution of the United States: Containing a Brief Commentary on Every Clause, Explaining the True Nature, Reasons, and Objects Thereof, Designed for the Use of School Libraries and General Readers.

Any reference to Justice Story's book is from a 2010 reprint by Harper Brothers, General Books, Memphis, Tennessee.

Justice Story made a point that an individual with an average education could fully understand our constitution. That only confirmed what I had learned from reading the Constitution and searching through it for information. Either Mr. Obama or Mr. Holder are reading their updated revisionist version, reprint number 201, or they failed to read it and simply attempted to hoodwink the listener.

Both Obama and Holder misled Governor Brewer, Article I, Section 10, Paragraph 3 is quite clear. If a threat is imminent, the governor may take necessary steps to "repel foreign invaders." Should uninvited illegal aliens from Mexico be considered "foreign invaders?" Absolutely, they were not invited and they are, though from nearby, foreign nevertheless.

Though the United States and Mexico are on friendly terms (which was not always the case) La Raza. La Raza is a Hispanic focus/activist organization claiming that all, or most of the territories ceded to the United State by the Treaty of Guadalupe-Hidalgo in 1848 remain the rightful property of Mexico. and President Felipe Calderon are under some misguided notion that the Treaty of Guadalupe Hidalgo—signed by both countries in 1848, ceded lands in question to the USA, and settled other boundaries—is invalid. That was the status quo until our government failed in its responsibilities and ceased rounding up and deporting all those without proper credentials.

Mr. Obama and Mr. Holder refuse to acknowledge one salient point relative to the multi-racial makeup of this great nation. All Americans have lived as a part of a multiracial demographic. No nation on earth has been as receptive to the immigration and full acceptance of foreigners into their midst. We recognize that, for the most part, immigrants have been a positive force in our economic strength and intellectual improvement.

Unfortunately, criminal and anti-social forces, socialism, fascism, communism, and fringe elements have been allowed to expectorate their poison of hate upon elements of our society.

So-called progressive education has allowed the most vulnerable of our society to be taught that our well-written Constitution demands separation of church and state. Such a notion is totally and completely antithetical to the beliefs of our founders. Nowhere in our constitution is there a phrase remotely suggesting a separation of church and state. To the contrary, the reverse is patently clear to any one capable of reading at the high school level.

The First Amendment *prohibits* the federal government from establishing a state religion and declares quite clearly that the government is *prohibited* from interfering in the people's religions. Yet even though biblical scenes are purposefully present in and on every one of our federal buildings, our Supreme Court has kowtowed to the likes of a Madalyn Murray O'Hair, the founder of American Atheists, and made the very presence of God in our classrooms impermissible. Our Puritan/Pilgrim ancestors made certain their children learned to read early on for the stated purpose that these children could not only read, but study the Bible.

There are those supposed scholars who propagate and perpetuate the falsehood that our great nation was *not* founded upon Christian principles.

The use of such nonsensical comments by his detractors, "George Washington was not a Christian, he was a Deist." are nonsensical, George Washington made it a point to attend different Christian church services—Episcopal, Presbyterian, Quaker, and others. It is further known (and evidence abounds) that General Washington frequently knelt in the presence of his troops and staff officers to ask God for guidance and protection in their endeavors.

The notion that Washington was not a Christian is dispelled by the narrations of many of his contemporaries reported in the great work of Benjamin F. Morris, "The Christian Life and Character of the Civil Institutions of the United States," Chapter 21, Publisher, American Vision, Powder Springs, Georgia. 2nd Ed, 2007.

Every patriot who signed the Declaration of Independence and every signatory of our Constitution was an announced believer in divine providence. Most were members of an active Christian congregation. For those readers concerned about the lack of any followers of Judaism, rest in peace. The first man to step forward to sign his name to protest the hated Stamp Act of the British Government was, the president of Mikve Israel Congregation (Philadelphia's only synagogue), Mathias Bush.

In the south, Francis Salvador, a Jew of Sephardic heritage—the first Jew to be elected to a Colonial constituent assembly—rode out to carry the alarm and raise the volunteers to repel impending Indians attacks. He returned at the head of a force of frontiersmen only to be ambushed, shot down, and scalped on July 1, 1776. Salvador had the honor of being the first American Jew to give his life for his adopted country.

Men such as Aaron Lopez were bankrupted supporting the Revolution, when their ships were lost to the British. In the area of finance, the young American government might have foundered too had it not been for the financial genius and personal financial risk and support taken on by Haym Solomon. Solomon was to die bankrupted by his total support of the American cause. Though small in number, the Jews chose to cast their fate with America.

Is it any wonder that in today's unsettled world, Israel is America's staunchest ally and we theirs. Our fates and fortunes are linked by solidarity of purpose and values, and a deep-rooted faith in God, or in YHWH (Yahweh) as he is known to the Jews.

A major thorn in the side of American society and culture is a practice best known as political correctness, or PC. This foolish and harmful deception dismisses homosexuals as "gay" and a learning disabled individual as a "moron." A blind individual is visually impaired, and a deaf-mute is deaf and dumb, he or she is hearing and speech impaired.

PC attempts to accommodate ethnic differences by euphemistically using hyphenated adjectives when describing American immigrants or Americans of mixed parentage, in an effort to ineptly make palatable that which may be—to the ignorant—unpalatable.

For instance, my spouse was born in Italy and immigrated into the United States in 1930. Never make the unsavory mistake of labeling her as *Italian-American*, or she will be all over you like sauce over spaghetti. She will let you know in no uncertain terms, "I am an American!" Hyphenated adjectives are an insult, inaccurate, and improper.

There exists a humanistic theory of evolution that propounds the theory that all humanity as we know it today is an extension of an evolution process that states *Homo sapiens* originated in Africa, and those earliest humans spread throughout the world.—The out-of-Africa theory. If one accepts that theory, by definition we are all *African Americans*; another misuse of totally incorrect and useless hyphenated ancestry.

In spite of the social programs begun by President John Kennedy in his New Frontier Agenda, and perpetuated by Lyndon Johnston in his Great Society agenda, civil (racial) unrest persisted. Racial segregation in the South was an abrasive that inflicted pain and unjustified torment upon black southerners.

Passage and ratification of the Fifteenth Amendment in 1870 gave all black males the vote. However, the Southern Democrats used intimidation to ensure the blacks voted as the Democratic Party wished. These untenable conditions persisted right up to the 1960s, and saw the beginnings of the civil rights movement and the devastation in black urban neighborhoods of New York City and Los Angeles, when race riots began in 1964.

By 1968, rioting had spread to hundreds of cities. This added to Johnson's troubles, which had already begun in Southeast Asia in 1963. By 1968, the Vietnam War overshadowed the programs of the Great Society and witnessed a huge conservative backlash. The devastation in black urban areas resulted in widespread lawlessness, and the use of illicit drugs gave rise to gang-related race wars. Troublemakers like Jesse Jackson and

Al Sharpton, rather than attempting to stem the tide of drugs and violence, vociferously and persistently blamed "whitey" for all the problems. Gang warfare over turf rights has proliferated rather than subsided and is a major problem with which we must deal. The Associated Press reported on December 29, 2012 in a publication *News One For Black America,* multiple instances of unprovoked, random homicides. The murder count reached 500 before the end of the year.

In spite of many serious negatives, America is still the nation of choice for foreign immigrants. The immigration of Muslims has begun to impact several areas in America. Muslims who insist upon retaining Sharia law must be reeducated, or forced to leave. America has been a most gracious host to many millions of peace-loving and law-abiding immigrants from virtually every nation in the world. If we are to retain and defend our hard-earned Christian heritage, every American—hyphenated or not— *must* insist that our constitution is and will continue to be the law of the land, and we are prepared to defend it by force of arms, if necessary. *Sharia* law has absolutely *no* place in America.

A major and undeniably cruel oversight in American history is the failure to make a much better use of the talents, wisdom, courage, and vitality of American womanhood. Anglo women first came to the American continent in 1608. They came at the behest of the first male colonists, who founded the Jamestown Colony on a land grant from the king of England. They married, gave birth to first generation

Americans, labored, fought alongside, and were and are still loyal Americans possessed of remarkable will and determination. Yet they remain gracious, feminine, and praiseworthy. America would and could not be America without them.

For all their good works, loyalty, and labor on behalf of our America, they have been systematically denied a full and equal partnership in this endeavor. They have been used, abused and not compensated to the extent they deserve. "It is possible, reading standard histories, to forget half the population of the country. The explorers were men, the landholders and merchants men, the political leaders men, the military figures men. The very invisibility of women, the overlooking of women, is a sign of their submerged status." [101] Zinn, Howard (2010-01-14). A People's History of the United States: 1492 to Present (p. 103). Harper Collins, Inc. Kindle Edition.

The conditions under which white settlers came to America created various situations for women. Where the first consisted almost entirely of men, women were imported as sex slaves, child bearers, companions. In 1619, the year that the first black indentured Africans came to Virginia, ninety English women arrived at Jamestown on one ship: "Agreeable persons, young and incorrupt...sold with their own consent to settlers as wives, the price to be the cost of their own transportation."[102] Many women came in those early years as indentured servants—often teenaged girls—and lived lives not much different from slaves, except that the term of service had an end. They were to be obedient to masters and mistresses.

The authors of America's Working Women (Baxandall, Gordon, and Reverby) describe the situation: [103]

> They were poorly paid and often treated rudely and harshly, deprived of good food and privacy. Of course these terrible conditions provoked resistance. Living in separate families without much contact with others in their position, indentured servants had one primary path of resistance open to them: passive resistance, trying to do as little work as possible and to create difficulties for their masters and mistresses. Of course, the masters and mistresses did not interpret it that way, but saw the difficult behavior of their servants as sullenness, laziness, malevolence, and stupidity. Ibid

The idea of women's suffrage in America had its seminal beginnings in Seneca Falls, New York, in 1848. With the passage of the aforementioned Fifteenth Amendment in 1870, women were again treated to second-class citizenship. It would take fifty long and arduous years before women were given the right to vote. Most women from Abigail Adams onward were of the correct opinion that they were "endowed by their Creator" with the same rights as their men. But even her husband, John, thought the idea laughable, which was despicable to say the least.

Two half-hearted—or rather lame—attempts were made by the two major parties when, in 1984, Walter Mondale, the Democratic presidential nominee chose as his running mate a self-proclaimed, hyphenated Italian-American, female lawyer-politician, and member of the US House of Representatives, Geraldine Ferraro. They were badly defeated, as expected in a landslide victory by incumbent Ronald Reagan and George H. W. Bush.

In 2008, the Republican nominee, John McCain, in an attempt to vitalize his lackluster campaign, chose the beautiful, vivacious, and extremely astute and politically savvy Sarah Palin, the sitting governor of Alaska, to be his running mate. That was the first time the Republicans had a female on the presidential ticket. The McCain-Palin ticket was defeated by the Obama-Biden ticket. McCain was really dead in the water because of his poor conservative record and a badly timed support for and involvement in Ted Kennedy's abortive illegal alien plan. McCain had, for all intents and purposes, become that pariah among conservatives: a RINO.

In summary, we the American people have failed to keep a critical eye on and to take immediate action to remove corrupt legislators, incompetent presidents, and failed to stem the growth of government. We lost our sense of morality and love of and faith in God. We allowed revisionist historian-educators to pass off untruths as fact. We have allowed fringe element of our society to play too big a role in our social mores and in our so-called entertainment venues.

More specifically, President Andrew Jackson should have been removed from office as should have Woodrow Wilson and Franklin D. Roosevelt, Jimmy Carter, William Jefferson Clinton and Barack Hussein Obama.

Members of the House of Representatives who have brought disrepute to that body and should have been removed are Alcee Hastings, Barney Frank, Charles Rangel, Maxine Waters, Nancy Pelosi, and Rush Holt. Many more may be guilty of dereliction of duty by not taking firm and decisive action against Barack Obama, for his failure to act in defense of those attacked in Benghazi on September 11, 2012, Eric Holder for his many High Crimes and Misdemeanors relative to Operation Fast and Furious, Jant Napolitano for her pompous refusal to give meaningful responses to members of Congress, regarding the purchase of million if not billions of rounds of hollow point ammunition and her utter lack of a reasonable attempt to deport a majority of some eleven million illegal aliens held in federal detention facilities and then turned loose in response to a feigned lack of funds to keep them incarcerated. Sequester they called it.

Both Nancy Pelosi and Rush Holt lied to the House Select Committee on Intelligence. Both stated the CIA had NOT told them about "waterboarding" Records of the CIA briefings show both had been briefed on that particular aspect of interrogation.

Every sitting Democratic senator is guilty of dereliction of duty, failing to honor his/her oath of office and, if a thorough investigation be done, all have likely been guilty of collusion with the imperial President Obama. They have individually and collectively followed the Party Line on legislation sent by the House of Representatives. In numerous cases there has not been one dissenting vote by a Democrat. As a result, no Budget has been forthcoming during Obama's tenure and this nation is over 16 Trillion dollars in debt; more than the previous 43 Administrations COMBINED! This is nearly an incomprehensible figure; however it comes out to $53,105.73 per citizen.

Furthermore, Congress has not taken any steps to shrink the bloated Washington bureaucracy and continues to give raises to, as they rate, the best workers huge bonuses and pay raises. The average government employee's salary and there are as of March 30, 2013, 21 million of them, is $123,049 per year. That is a whopping $2,584,029,000,000 (over 2 Trillion per year). We are in over our eyebrows. Can Momma prepare a budget and get us out of this mess? If she can't, there goes our republic to which Ben Franklin alluded in 1797. I am betting a female president can get us turned around. Right, Mom?

When I set about writing this piece, I had no notion to make it a rant or to rail against fate. There is no fiction included, simply facts as I know them, and my own conservative observations in judgment of those facts. I have been observing the best and the worst this great country has had to offer for some eight decades.

Of one thing I am absolutely certain: the good ol' boy politics that have plagued this wonderful country for two hundred plus years must be diluted, modified, or abolished. We must get all the American people involved. We absolutely must clamp down on any behaviors that run counter to our Judeo-Christian ethos. If we have not the will and the patience to do so, the republic we have held for so short a time will disappear into the dustbin of history. That is so sad a thought.

Therefore, this old man's single agenda—until Father Time takes his toll—is to do all in my power to effect the election of two American ladies to the offices of president and vice president of the United States of America. It is a lofty and necessary goal if we are to survive as a democratic republic. God willing, 2016 is as good a time as any.

While assembling this piece, I kept in mind all those great ladies who dedicated their most valiant efforts to the cause of equality for women, specifically Alice Paul, Susan B. Anthony, Lucretia Mott, Vida Ann Kerr, Pearl Etha Williams, Inez E. Hupp, and others. Also, I kept in mind as highly eligible presidential candidates the following: Michele Bachmann, Sarah Palin, Penny Nance, Frances Rice, Kay Bailey Hutchison, Jean Schmidt, Cynthia Lummis, Shelley Capito, Cathy McMorris Rodgers, Condoleeza Rice, and Jan Brewer.

At this point, I should like to ask, rhetorically, why has America never had a female chief executive? America has showed the rest of the world that we are an *exceptional* people. Yet we have failed to keep step with other less accomplished nations. Many nations, fifty-seven at least, have opted for a woman to lead their government. As of today, in other countries there are twenty elected or appointed female heads of government.

The answer, quite simply and with some rancor, is either misogyny, gynophobia, or simply a built in gender bias. Not too long back, I was watching *Jeopardy!* and Alex Trebek asked a young female contestant what she wanted to do when she grew up. Her immediate and positive response was "I am going to be president of the United States." She was obviously not aware of the status quo. I am on her side; I hope she makes it.

There is some movement to empower women. On August 13, 2012, at a congress held in Seoul, South Korea, Secretary General Ban ki-Moon of the United Nations said, "The empowerment of young women is key for advancing development around the world" and added that it is a priority for the United Nations to encourage their active participation in society. "The lack of women's representation—of women's empowerment—affects individual women's rights— and it holds back whole countries," Mr. Ban told participants at the First World Congress of Global Partnership for Young Women and Second Global Partnership Forum.

"From farming to leading governments and troops, women have repeatedly shown that they can excel in many areas and make positive contributions to their countries," Mr. Ban said. However, he noted that they still do not enjoy the same benefits as men, and called on "governments to support their advancement."

The gender bias is but one major problem that has become firmly entrenched in American politics.

Women might take a cue from the Greek playwright Aristophanes, who authored two plays on the theme of gender differences in the fifth century B.C.. In the play *Lysistrata*, the title character suggested to the ladies of Athens that they withhold sexual favors from their husband and lovers in an effort to force the men to stop the Peloponnesian War.

Well, I have spoken much about what got us to this point. Now, I offer a few words from an old man who loves this great country and prays nightly for its survival. God does work in mysterious ways. I choose not to question His methods. I accept that He has a path along, which we are destined to find our way. Forks in that road demand a decision. He knows what that decision will be. We must make the proper decisions, difficult though they may be.

I suggest we take a look back and see what our forebears did to set us upon this thorny path. They had no intentions but good for their descendants, too many of whom strayed and introduced far too many of Satan's playthings. Newspapers were the first; they offered us a particular view on many happenings, particularly political. For instance, they informed us of the promises of each and every presidential candidate. "A chicken in every pot and a car in every garage." No, Herbert Hoover did *not* say that. However, it was reported that he did. Though not particularly accurate, the *New York Times* claims that the newspaper was the first popular and national medium for "All the News That's Fit to Print," now the motto of the *Times.*

The human animal is so gullible and possessed of such childlike trust; when even the most preposterous items were reported as news, we fell for it hook, line, and sinker.

America has made tremendous use of the communications media: newspapers, telephones, radio, and that monster, television. For the first few years that television existed in its uniqueness, it was quite loveable. Many entertainers became household names, were paid handsomely, and for the most part, were welcomed as part of the family. From such luminaries as Red Skelton, Carol Burnett, and Rod Serling; entertainment was the goal. They succeeded admirably as did musical entertainers like Lawrence Welk, Nat King Cole and Grand Ol'Opry. And none of them ever said a foul word.

That all changed with Richard Pryor, Redd Foxx, and Lenny Bruce; all of whom used foul language to the extreme. They had a huge following, but their material became jaded and totally filthy. Many were admitted users of hard drugs, which led some really misguided youths and middle-aged viewers to experiment and eventually become hooked. Most recently, television advertisements for erectile dysfunction aids are shown numerous times each day. Children of all ages are viewers. One youngster when asked to define resurrection remarked, "If you get one that lasts over four hours, call the doctor." That may seem amusing, but it is a symptom of a debilitating and possibly fatal illness in our country.

Homosexuality is a sin, that fact seems not to faze nor deter many in the really sick entertainment jungle. There was a time not so long ago when gay men and lesbian women were seemingly content to remain closeted. Mr. and Mrs. God-fearing-and-God-loving-Main-Street America respected that desirability for anonymity. Then came the Haight-Ashbury let-it-all-hang-out freaks demanding special recognition and a claim for special rights. Ellen DeGeneres, a self-proclaimed lesbian was signed to a contract to have her own one-lesbian show. Later, she announced in 2008 that she and her lover, Portia De Rossi, were getting married. That ended when De Rossi reportedly changed her mind about having a baby by artificial insemination or through natural means.

For this sideshow, DeGeneres is reportedly worth some $90 million. What a horrible change in our sense of values. Sir Elton John—who is seen by some as a fantastic musician—is a self-proclaimed homosexual, married to another of the same persuasion. Their adoption of a baby boy could appear to be an absolute perversion and a danger to the future welfare of the child. Somewhere along the line, we as a decent and humane society, must take a stand and eliminate homosexuality, simply because God created man and woman for the purpose of procreation, impossible in a homosexual relationship or a one-night stand.

Recently, CNN's Anderson Cooper stated that he is gay and always has been. He joined CNN's Don Lemon and Salon's Steve Kornacki, MSNB.C.'s Rachel Maddow and Thomas Roberts, and Jane Velez-Mitchell of HLN. "He's a role model to millions and now will inspire countless others," said Herndon Graddick, the president of the Gay and Lesbian Alliance Against Defamation, a media advocacy group."

To me, one cannot defame the infamous, nor belittle the scornful. This wonderful nation has provided so much for so many, and yet we have allowed the lowest common denominator to dictate or at least to have a more-than-earned say in how we conduct business. The malefactors are reaping rewards inconsistent with their value to society. Our tasteless president has expressed a decided preference for the gay lifestyle, surrounded himself with those of the same persuasion, cancelled the presidentially decreed "Day of Prayer" and substituted a Muslim day of prayer celebrated it in *our* Judeo-Christian White House. His effrontery and his callous disregard for centuries of Christian practice is nauseating.

Homosexuality and bestiality are now permissible in our military. Marriage as prescribed by law as between one man and one woman, and set forth in public law as DOMA is not being enforced by Obama and Holder. For this, they should be impeached. Our 112th Congress is, and has been, dysfunctional. Every member of this Congress is in violation of their oath of office, and by their very actions, are a collusive body in commission of numerous high crimes and misdemeanors, not the least of which is treason.

All the aforementioned conduct is offensive to Him who bestowed upon this nation His blessings. We have become so jaded in our choices of entertainment and entertainers. We laugh at the filthy jokes and the silly primping and the outlandish clothing. God is certainly keeping tally, for our reminder. He needs no reminder, He knows and remembers all our transgressions and violations of His commandments.

Allow me now to address the subject of gender bias. Are men and women equal in the eyes of God? Many theologians and Bible scholars insist that God made man superior to woman. Why? Eve seduced Adam to eat the forbidden fruit! "I will increase your pain and your labor when you give birth to children. Yet, you will long for your husband, and he will rule you." Gen 3,16 Baker Publishing Group (2010-07-16). Holy Bible, GOD'S WORD Translation (GW) (with direct verse lookup and book and chapter navigation) (Kindle Locations 303-305). Baker Book Group. Kindle Edition.

Thereafter, Adam proclaimed, "Eve made me do it!"

"In the marriage drama the players are husband and wife. Each has a role to depict. The husband portrays Christ and the wife represents the church. Nothing could be clearer than this in Scripture: "For a husband is in charge of his wife in the same way Christ is in charge of his body the church... So you wives must willingly obey your husbands in everything, just as the church obeys Christ. And you husbands, show the same kind of love to your wives as Christ showed to the church when he died for her..." [99]

From this old man's point of view, and with eighty years of observation, Jesus was most persuasive when he acted contrary to accepted Jewish law and practiced a change in status. Jesus' treatment of women was revolutionary.

Christ overthrew many centuries of Jewish law and custom. He consistently treated women and men as equals. He violated numerous Old Testament regulations, which specified gender inequality. He refused to follow the behavioral rules established by the three main Jewish religious groups of the day: the Essenes, Pharisees, and Sadducees. The actions of Jesus of Nazareth towards women were therefore revolutionary.

Revolutionary appears to be a most appropriate choice of words. The actions of the American people— we the people—will need to be revolutionary if we desire to achieve the status we so richly deserve. Our forebears put us on the right course. We set standards of excellence unmatched in the world. However, we have gone into a steady and sickening decline in behavior, morality, generosity, trust, courtesy, loyalty, thrift, cleanliness, and above all, Godliness.

Our mothers did their very best. Absentee, deadbeat dads and their slothful offspring who are so utterly dependent on social welfare are a blight upon this great nation. It is high time to make an about face, elect Mom to establish a budget, set higher moral standards and a cleaner, healthier way of life. The Good Old Boys have failed, miserably.

Election Day, November 2016, must be the day we make the big change.

AFTERWORD

I did not come into possession of this work by W. Leon Skousen until I was well along with my book. Most certainly it deserves more than an epilogue. Therefore, I shall attempt to do justice to Dr. Skousen's authoritative *the Five Thousand Year Leap*. I first heard about the book listening to a Glenn Beck broadcast.

Dr. Skousen began work on this larger-than-life examination of that which he so aptly named "A Miracle That Changed the World."

He started in the 1930s while attending law school, worked on the book for the next fifty years, and finally published it in 1981. My copy was copyrighted in 1991, 2006 by the National Center for Constitutional Studies, and my copy is of the nineteenth edition published by that organization.

The Five Thousand Year Leap is well-indexed and brilliantly researched, which allowed Dr. Skousen to present a valid testament to the worth of the Constitution of the United States.

Our founders had, in many instances, studied the same authors and documents as did Dr. Skousen.

Dr. Skousen laid out the twenty-eight principles followed by the founders in writing our rather abbreviated, but absolutely thorough, complete, and specific document of governance. The ten amendments making up the Bill of Rights were necessary. The seventeen since have not been so commendable. I shall list these twenty-eight principles for the readers' edification and commend to them the entire brilliance of Dr. Skousen's insightful and uplifting work.

THE TWENTY-EIGHT PRINCIPLES

Quoted precisely as presented in *the Five Thousand Year Leap*

1. The only reliable basis for sound government and just human relations is natural law.

2. A free people cannot survive under a republican constitution unless they remain virtuous and morally strong.

3. The most promising method of securing a virtuous and morally stable people is to elect virtuous leaders.

4. Without religion, the government of a free people cannot be maintained.

5. All things were created by God, therefore upon him all mankind are equally dependent, and to him they are equally responsible.

6. All men are created equal.

7. The proper role of government is to protect equal rights, not provide equal things.

8. Men are endowed by their Creator with certain unalienable rights.

9. To protect man's rights, God has revealed certain principles of divine law.

10. The God-given right to govern is vested in the sovereign authority of the whole people.

11. The majority of the people may alter or abolish a government which has become tyrannical.

12. The United States of America shall be a republic.

13. A constitution should be structured to permanently protect the people from the human frailties of their rulers.

14. Life and liberty are secure only so long as the right to property is secure.

15. The highest level of prosperity occurs when there is a free-market economy and a minimum of government regulations.

16. The government should be separated into three branches—legislative, executive, and judicial.

17. A system of checks and balances should be adopted to prevent the abuse of power.

18. The unalienable rights of the people are most likely to be preserved if the principles of government are set forth in a written constitution.

19. Only limited and carefully defined powers should be delegated to government, all others being retained in the people.

20. Efficiency and dispatch require government to operate according to the will of the majority, but constitutional provisions must be made to protect the rights of the minority.

21. Strong local self-government is the keystone to preserving human freedom.

22. A free people should be governed by law and not by the whims of men.

23. A free society cannot survive as a republic without a broad program of general education.

24. A free people will not survive unless they stay strong.

25. "Peace, commerce, and honest friendship with all nations—entangling alliances with none."

26. The core unit which determines the strength of any society is the family; therefore, the government should foster and protect its integrity.

27. The burden of debt is as destructive to freedom as subjugation by conquest.

28. The United States has a manifest destiny to be an example and a blessing to the entire human race.

"Breathes there the man with soul so dead, Who never to himself hath said, This is my Own, my native land! Whose heart hath ne'er within him burned, As home his footstep he hath turned from wandering on a foreign strand?"

Sir Walter Scott; "Lay of the Last Minstrel", Canto vi, St 1

Various (2009-10-04). Familiar Quotations (Kindle Locations 1343-1345). Public Domain Books. Kindle Edition.

ENDNOTES

1   "Jackson Hole Historical Society and Museum." http://www.jacksonholehistory.org/history/characters/

2   Colin Nickerson. "Oregon cave yields evidence of the earliest Americans yet." *Boston Globe*. http://www.boston.com/news/nation/articles/2008/04/04/oregon_cave_yields_evidence_of_the_earliest_americans_yet/?page=full

3   "Last Glacial Period." Wikipedia. http://en.wikipedia.org/wiki/Last_glacial_period

4   "Wisconsin Glaciation." Zonu.com. http://www.zonu.com/detail-en/2009-11-09-10972/Wisconsin-glaciation.html

5   New York: Sackett & Wilhelms Litho. Co, 1891.

6   Wilbur R. Jacobs. "Tip of the Iceberg,' *William and Mary Quarterly*, 3 Ser, Vol 31, no. No. 1, 1974.

7   P. Scaruffi. *A Timeline of Roman Empire*, 1999.

8   Christianity in View, "Timeline of Christina History." http://www.christianityinview.com/timeline.html

9   Lutheran Church of the Resurrection. "Timeline of the Protestant Reformation." http://www.lcr-yardley.org/content/adulted/ProtestantReformation.pdf

10 American Studies of the University of Virginia. "Context and Developments." http://xroads. virginia.edu/~CAP/PURITAN/purhist.html

11 "The Mayflower Contact." http://mayflowerhistory. com/PrimarySources/MayflowerCompact.php

12 Edward Winslow. "How The Pilgrims Lived." The National Center for Public Policy Research. http:// www.nationalcenter.org/Pilgrims.html

13 "The Pilgrims' First Thanksgiving." Hubbard's Cupboard. http://www.hubbardscupboard.org/ the_pilgrims__first_thanksgivi.html

14 William Bradford. *Of Plymouth Plantation, 1620– 1647*, ed. by S. E. Morison, 1952.

15 "English Colonial Era 1700 to 1763." The History Place. http://www.historyplace.com/unitedstates/ revolution/rev-col.htm

16 "Declaratory Act." Encyclopedia Britannica. http:// www.britannica.com/EB.C.hecked/topic/155205/ Declaratory-Act

17 "The Townshend Revenue Act." ushistory.org. http://www.ushistory.org/declaration/related/ townshend.htm

18 Nathaniel Kapner. "Woodrow Wilson–Pawn of the Jews." Real Jews News.

19 "Alice Paul: Feminist, Suffragist and Political Strategist." Alice Paul Institute. http://www. alicepaul.org/alicepaul.htm

20 Bob Diamond. "Woodrow Wilson–Peck's Bad Boy." Aventura News. http://www.communitynewspapers.com/aventura/woodrow-wilson-peck's-bad-boy/

21 "President Wilson Blackmailed." sweetliberty.org. http://www.sweetliberty.org/issues/hoax/unt.htm

22 http://www.realjewnews.com/p=189

23 http://www.youtube.com/watch?v=gxISjdbLjhA

24 "How the Jews Bought Woodrow Wilson." *VNN Forum.* July 2007. http://vnnforum.com/showthread.php?t=69072

25 "Wilson nominates Brandeis to the Supreme Court." history.com. http://www.history.com/this-day-in-history/wilson-nominates-brandeis-to-the-supreme-court

26 Nathanael Kapner. "Woodrow Wilson Pawn of the Zionists." Tin Foil Hat News. http://tinfoil-hat-news.blogspot.com/2010/08/woodrow-wilson-pawn-of-zionists.html

27 http://www.sweetliberty.org/issues/hoax/unt.htm

28 "Calvin Coolidge." whitehouse.gov. http://www.whitehouse.gov/about/presidents/calvincoolidge

29 "President Roosevelt versus the U.S. Supreme Court!!" Reformation Online. http://www.reformation.org/supreme-court.html

30 *"Truman on Israel."* http://www.youtube.com/watch?v=IYdGcojkMD0

31 "President Harry S. Truman and US Support for Israeli Statehood." MidEastWeb. http://mideastweb.org/us_supportforstate.htm

32 http://www.trumanlibrary.org/photos/israel.jpg

33 "Harry S. Truman." whitehouse.gov. http://www.whitehouse.gov/about/presidents/harrystruman

34 http://b-29s-over-korea.com/Why-Truman-Fired-General-MacArthur/Why-Truman-Fired-General-MacArthur

35 "Lyndon B Johnson." whitehouse.gov. http://www.whitehouse.gov/about/presidents/lyndonbjohnson

36 "How did the Vietnam War start?" WikiAnswers. http://wiki.answers.com/Q/How_did_the_Vietnam_War_start

37 "Jimmy Carter." whitehouse.gov. http://www.whitehouse.gov/about/presidents/jimmycarter

38 http://www.history.com/topics/911attacks/videos?mkwid=suqXBfh0J_pcrid_8838840918_pkw_september%2011%202001%20terrorism_pmt_b#911-timeline

39 "Barack Obama." whitehouse.gov. http://www.whitehouse.gov/about/presidents/barackobama

40 http://www.digitalhistory.uh.edu/database/article_display.cfm?HHID=6

41 "Political Parties Quotes." Schmoop. http://www.shmoop.com/political-parties/quotes.html

42 http://www.bartleby.com/73/1593.htm

43 "Andrew Jackson." whitehouse.gov. http://www.whitehouse.gov/about/presidents/andrewjackson

44 "Snow Job and Bill Clinton." American Patriot Friends Network. http://www.apfn.org/apfn/snowjob.htm

45 "Bill Clinton's Skeleton Closet." The Skeleton Closet. http://www.relchange.org/clinton.htm

46 "Political Corruption." Wikipedia. http://en.wikipedia.org/wiki/Political_corruption

47 "Milestones in the History of Media and Politics." Public Broadcasting Service. http://www.pbs.org/now/politics/mediahistory.html

48 "The New England Courant." Wikipedia. http://en.wikipedia.org/wiki/The_New_England_Courant

49 "Andrew Jackson: An American President." Public Broadcasting Service. http://www.pbs.org/kcet/andrewjackson/edu/domesticpolicy.html

50 "Female World Leaders Currently In Power." Filibuster Cartoons. http://www.filibustercartoons.com/charts_rest_female-leaders.php

51 "Ban: leadership of young women crucial to advance development worldwide." United Nations News Center. http://www.un.org/apps/news/story.asp?NewsID=42675

52 "Lysistrata." Wikipedia. http://en.wikipedia.org/wiki/Lysistrata

53 Brian Stelter. "Revelation Signals a Shift in Views of Homosexuality." *The New York Times.* http://mediadecoder.blogs.nytimes.com/2012/07/02/anderson-cooper-says-the-fact-is-im-gay/

54 B.A. Robinson. "Women's roles in the Bible." Religious Tolerance. http://www.religioustolerance.org/cfe_bibl.htm

55 Howard Zinn. *A People's History of the United States 1492 to present.* New York: Harper Collins, Inc., 2010, 103.

56 National Park Service, "The Indispensable Role of Women at Jamestown." Accessed May 19, 2013. http://www.nps.gov/jame/historyculture/the-indispensible-role-of-women-at-jamestown.htm.

WORKS REFERENCED

A. E. Wood. *At the Foot of the Flatiron.* American Mutoscope and Biograph Co., 1903. 35mm film, from Library of Congress, *The Life of a City: Early Films of New York, 1898–1906*, MPEG video, 2:19. http://lcweb2.loc.gov/ammem/papr/nychome.html

John Harwood. "The Pros and Cons of Biden." *New York Times.* Video, 2:00. http://video.on.nytimes.com/?fr_story=a425c9aca92f51bd19f2a621fd93b5e266507191.

Michael Pollan. "Michael Pollan Gives a Plant's-Eye View." March 2007. TED video, 17:31. http://www.ted.com/index.php/talks/michael_pollan_gives_a_plant_s_eye_view.html